# The Sun is Always Shining

Renewing your heart and mind
through the Light of Christ

Ryan J. Hulbert, Ph.D.

ISBN-13: 978-1512284843
ISBN-10: 151228484X

To Theresa, my wife and best friend,
and to our wonderful children
David
John
Daniel
Stephen
Benjamin
Marijke
Sarai

As one who has worked in the fields of education, religion, and counseling, I found Dr. Ryan Hulbert's book, *The Sun Is Always Shining,* about 20 years ago. It is a clear, practical, yet profound resource for helping persons work their way, beyond all the hindrances which can derail the journey, toward wholeness and higher levels of well being. I highly recommend it.


Dr. Virgil A. Wood

Dr. Virgil A. Wood
2428 Ameno Drive, Pearland, TX 77581
281-464-3822  email: drwood@soulscope.com  websites -
freethedream.org  and  becauseallivesmatter.net

Dr. Wood, Church leader, educator, and civil rights activist, has committed much of his life's work to the struggle for economic, educational and spiritual development among the nation's disadvantaged.

A Pastor for over 50 years in the states of Virginia, Massachusetts, and Rhode Island, he retired from active Pastoral Ministry in 2005, and became a resident of Pearland, Texas.

He served with Martin Luther King, Jr., as a member of his National Executive Board of the Southern Christian Leadership Conference for the last ten years of Dr. King's life and work, and coordinated the State of Virginia in the Historic March on Washington on April 28, 1963.

He received his Doctorate in Education from Harvard University, where two of his major Professors were Organization Development Expert, Dr. Chris Argyris, and Achievement Motivation Expert, Dr. David McClellan. He graduated from Virginia Union University and Andover Newton Theological School. As an educator, he served as Dean and Director of the African American Institute, and Associate Professor of Northeastern University at Boston, and had been a Professor at Virginia Seminary and College, in Lynchburg, and a visiting Lecturer, Research and Teaching Fellow at Harvard University.

Among his publications are the *Introduction to Black Church Economic Studies*, (Sparks Press; Raleigh, N.C., 1974) originator and contributing editor of, *The Jubilee Bible*, (American Bible Society, New York, 1999, and reissued in 2012) and author of, *In Love We Trust: Lessons I Learned From Martin Luther King*, (published by Beckham House, Silver Spring, Maryland, 2005). He has combined his dual career in Church Leadership and Education with a life-long commitment to community development and economic and spiritual transformation.

## About the Author

Ryan J Hulbert, Ph.D., graduated from Brigham Young University, and received his doctorate in clinical psychology from the University of Nebraska-Lincoln, with sub-specialties in alcoholism treatment and rural community mental health. In 1986, he completed a research fellowship at the Catholic University of Louvain, Belgium where his fascination with the role of time perspective in human functioning began.

Dr. Hulbert served as a staff psychologist and Director of Research at the Cherokee Mental Health Institute in Cherokee, Iowa between 1988 and 1993. He was the Chief Psychologist of BPA Behavioral Health for 8 years, and was the Clinical Services Administrator for the Idaho Department of Juvenile Corrections from 2001-2009. In 2010, he assisted in the initial program development for the Management & Training Corporation's Correctional Alternative Placement Program (CAPP), in Idaho. Beginning in 2015 he has taught psychology courses as an adjunct faculty member at Boise State University, and is the Clinical Director at Abundance Behavioral Health Services in Caldwell, Idaho.

He is the author of several articles in professional journals, has presented numerous workshops, and is the author of the books, The Sun Is Always Shining, Drivers' Ed for the Brain, Growth Rings, and Eternity Time Eternity. He is also the inventor of The Youth Support Team Game.

He is the founder of EPIC Psychological Services, with "EPIC" being an acronym for "Empowering People in Communities." His professional mission is to lighten the darkness, warm the hearts, and increase the agency of his clients, colleagues, and community. He views his strengths as compassion, creativity, and enthusiasm, in working with others to enhance health and reduce human suffering through increasingly effective, accessible, and cost effective methods.

He and his wife, Theresa, have 5 sons, 2 daughters, 4 daughters-in-law, 1 son-in-law, and a growing number of grandchildren. They live in the country near Parma, Idaho. Dr. Hulbert very much enjoys spending time with his family, fishing, helping others, and doing family history research.

# ACKNOWLEDGEMENTS

I would like to express appreciation to Bill Pettit, M.D., who provided much inspiration in viewing people as being naturally healthy, and at times needing guidance to begin to realize their natural strength. His wife, Sue Pettit kindly gave permission to use her poems, "Lillie's Loose" and "Thunderdrops & Raindrops. Kate Blake, Director of Marketing of MCC Behavioral Care, was very helpful in obtaining permission to use the picture on the book cover. The diagrams which include the "perception veil" were adapted from diagrams in Joe Bailey's book, *The Serenity Principle*. Format suggestions and final production of diagrams were made by Lenora O'Brien.

I especially want to thank my wife and children for their help and patience through this process. In addition to much advice, my wife Theresa typed the manuscript. My research mentor, Willy Lens, at the Catholic University of Louvain, Belgium first introduced me to the intriguing and powerful role of time perspective in human functioning. The original self printed manuscript, in 1996, was shared with family, friends, clients, and other professionals. I am grateful that they found it helpful during the last 20 years. Rochelle Fowler prepared the manuscript for this printing, Stephen Hulbert provided helpful review and comments, and Marjike Grant designed the front and back cover.

The development of this book was a wonderful personal experience for me. It allowed me to focus on Jesus Christ, the source of all healing, and to bring his influence more directly into psychotherapy.

# Table of Contents

# SECTION I

# Introduction

In February 1992, I was in the Minneapolis Airport, preparing for a short flight to the Omaha Airport. Having lived in northwest Iowa for several years, I had become accustomed to the bitter cold February winters in the Midwest. I was not accustomed, however, to flying in such weather. It was a dreary, dark, overcast day with sleet falling. A small 15-seat plane approached the gate where I was waiting, and it became obvious that this was the plane that I would take to Omaha. I began feeling nervous about flying in such weather in a small plane. I bundled up to cross the few yards to the airplane and climbed aboard.

The roar of the plane's engines added to my sense of tension, as we began taxiing down the runway. After we took off from the runway, it seemed that we were traveling upward at an especially steep angle. All of a sudden, in the midst of traveling through the dark gray cloud cover, the plane pierced the cloud cover and burst into a startling realm of light.

I was startled by the blueness of the sky and looked up to see the sun shining brightly, as if it was a summer day. After being deeply impressed by this for a few minutes, I looked down toward the ground. Sure enough, there was the dark cloud cover. At that moment the thought occurred to me, *The people down there don't know the sun is shining!* In fact, *I* hadn't known until only moments before. I enjoyed the blue sky and the sunshine for only about twenty minutes before the gradual descent into the Omaha airport, where once again I slipped below the clouds into the wintry world. So profound was the experience in the sunshine that I was able to remember that the sun was still shining.

Since that experience, it has occurred to me that the sun is <u>always</u> shining. We live on an earth which rotates on its axis, allowing us to have the perception that the sun has gone down, when in actuality, it continues to burn brightly while we are the experiencing darkness. We learn many things by experiencing their opposites, and without the experience of being away from the light for a time, we could never experience the welcome rays of the sun as it "comes up" each morning.

During the daylight hours, when clouds come over, we have the experience of not seeing the sun. Just a few Saturdays ago, I looked out the window and saw the gray sky and heard myself say, "Oh, I wish the sun was shining today." I had to remind myself that it was, in fact shining, but that I wasn't able to experience its full effect at the time. Somehow, it was comforting, even though the skies remained gray, that the sun was really up there.

1

When I was above the clouds in the bright sunshine, that was reality. When I was below the clouds in the darkness, that was also reality. Having gone from the clouds into the sunlight, the higher reality allowed me to comprehend what was going on both above and below the clouds. The experience of being only below the clouds, was a more limited reality that did not allow for a full appreciation of what was in the sunshine. In other words, the lower reality had a ceiling effect, limiting the fuller perspective and comprehension of the whole truth. It is as if the ceiling of our current awareness allows us to understand only the amount of truth on our current level of light and below, but does not allow us to fully comprehend truths above our current level of light (see Diagram 1).

In this book, I will attempt to convey a number of concepts and techniques, which have greatly helped me and my clients to have a less limiting and more joyful perspective on life. Since we all experience ups and down in life, I have found it extremely helpful to better understand at what elevation I am at any given time. In other words, it can be helpful to have a reading on our level of "upness" to then know how much of the full perspective and whole truth we are experiencing. If we are low, and know we are low, then we can realize that what we currently perceive is a more limited view, and thus be less trapped by the limited perspective and truth.

# Diagram 1

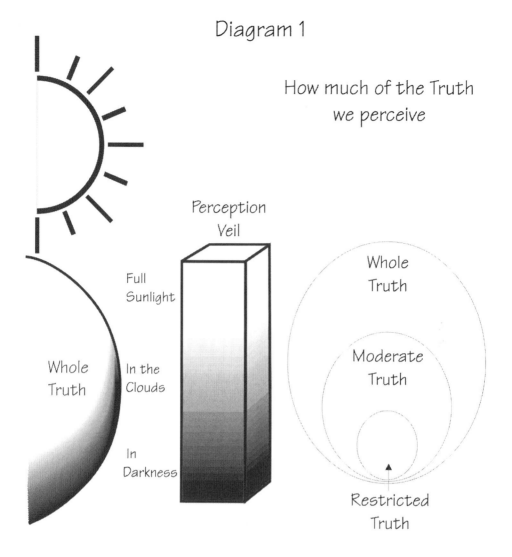

How much of the Truth
we perceive

Perception
Veil

Full
Sunlight

Whole
Truth

In the
Clouds

In
Darkness

Whole
Truth

Moderate
Truth

Restricted
Truth

"Then I saw that wisdom excelleth folly, as far as light excelleth darkness.

The wise man's eyes are in his head; but the fool walketh in darkness:  and I myself perceived also that one event happeneth to them all."

Ecclesiastes 2:13, 14

I will attempt to carefully describe a number of vertical levels of experience, each in a variety of ways, with the hope that the reader can identify with, at least, several of the characteristics of each level. These characteristics can then serve as elevation/perspective/truth indicators, almost like instruments on the panel of an airplane for navigation.

The first and most basic characteristic of the levels of truth is that of a continuum from light to dark. Although this continuum actually has many shades as it goes from dark through the gray to the light, for the sake of simplicity, three basic levels will be discussed. These levels correspond with three degrees of light. It can be described as "sunshine," "cloudy," and "dark." The increasing amount of light corresponds to increased wisdom, insight, clarity and true perspective.

In each portion of the book, a principle will be stated, accompanied by supporting scripture verses, and followed by further discussion or practical examples. As the book progresses, the descriptions of the levels of truth are further elaborated, according to the principle being discussed.

*Jesus said, "I am the way, the truth, and the life:*
*no man cometh unto the Father, but by me."*
St. John 14:6
*"Then spoke Jesus again unto them, saying, I am the light of the world;*
*he that followeth me shall not walk in darkness,*
*but shall have the light of life."*
St. John 8:12

The more spiritual light we are receiving the more truly alive we are and the more truthful our perspective and awareness. The basic purpose of this book is to assist in better discerning which of our perceptions are more truthful, according to the amount of light and aliveness we are experiencing at the time of the perceptions. Through being thus better equipped, we can begin to pay more attention to truths and less attention to untruths. I have found that through this process I am better able to recognize truths and more clearly identify untruths. As we experience greater light, areas of darkness stand out, and become more obvious because of the contrast.

# Chapter 1

## The Son is Always Shining

Principle 1:   JESUS CHRIST'S LOVE FOR EACH OF US NEVER DIMINISHES.

> *"It is of the Lord's mercies that we are not consumed,*
> *because His compassions fail not.  They are new every morning."*
> Lamentations 3:22-23

I would like to compare the fact that the sun is always shining to the fact that the Son is truly always shining.  Or, in other words, the love of the Son of God, Jesus Christ, is always warm and bright in our behalf.  What does change, however, is our degree of experiencing that love and warmth, just like when clouds or darkness lessen the experience of feeling the warmth or seeing the light of the sun.  When we more fully comprehend the assurance that Christ's love for us truly never diminishes, many of the confusing aspects of life can be better dealt with, and thus can better contribute to our growth and development.  When we are not fully experiencing the warmth and love of Jesus Christ, it usually has to do with our individual level of perspective at that moment (see Diagram 2).

Principle 2:   WE KNOW SOMETHING BEST BY EXPERIENCING ITS OPPOSITE.

> *"For ye were sometimes darkness, but now are ye light in the Lord:*
> *walk as children of light."*
> Ephesians 5:8
> *"Wherefore he saith, Awake thou that sleepest,*
> *and arise from the dead, and Christ shall give thee light."*
> Ephesians 5:14

# Diagram 2

What we Experience

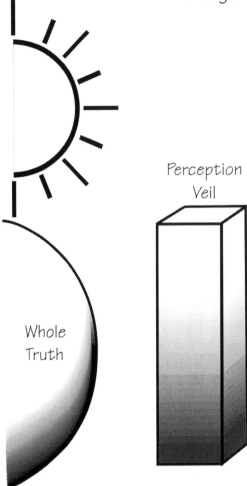

Perception
Veil

Feeling
Christ's
Love for
Us

Not Feeling
Christ's
Love
for
Us

Whole
Truth

"That they may know from the rising of the sun, and from the west, that there is none beside me. I am the Lord, and there is none else."

Isaiah 45:6

"I will never leave thee, nor forsake thee."

Hebrews 13:5

Although there is much darkness of spirit and mind in the world in which we live, the Savior has come to help us both understand the difference between light and darkness, and learn to not stay in the darkness. In order to allow for real faith to be exercised by us, it is at times necessary that we *not* experience the light. In St. John 1:5 we read, "And the light shineth in darkness; and the darkness comprehended it not." We could never develop real trust if things always made sense, just as we could never develop real courage, if victory was always obvious. Belief in the light, even when it is not readily apparent, is necessary to eventually fully appreciate it. In John 12:46, we read, "I am come a light into the world, that whosoever believeth on me should not abide in darkness." Similarly, Isaiah declared (Isaiah 9:2) "The people that walked in darkness have seen a great light; they that dwell in the land of the shadow of death, upon them hath the light shined."

Christ descended below all darkness when he suffered and atoned for our sins. The prophet Daniel stated (Daniel 2:22), "he knoweth what is in the darkness, and the light dwelleth with him." Christ not only has the power to support us in times of darkness and to cleanse us from all mistakes, He has the personal knowledge of what we're going through, from His own experience and therefore knows how to heal us: "...the Sun of righteousness arise with healing in his wings..." (Malachi 4:2)

Principle 3: JESUS CHRIST IS THE SOURCE OF LIGHT AND TRUTH IN AND FOR ALL PEOPLE.

> *"All things were made by Him, and without Him was not*
> *anything made that was made...that was the true Light which*
> *lighteneth every man that cometh into the world."*
> St. John 1:3,9
> *"But there is a spirit in man: and the inspiration of the*
> *Almighty giveth them understanding."*
> Job 32:8

Speaking about the creation, Moses wrote in the first chapter in the book of Genesis (verses 16-18): "And God made two great lights; the greater light to rule the day and the lesser light to rule the night: He made the stars also. And God set them in the firmament of the heaven to give light upon the earth, and to rule over the day and over the night, and to divide the light from the darkness: and God saw that it was good." We see from the above verses, that there is a purpose for both light and darkness, and that even in darkness, we are not left alone without the influence of, at least, some light. The lesser lights can serve as guides, but their relative

7

dimness also allows us to greatly appreciate the contrast of the greater light that rules the day.

In further examining Christ, as our source of light, John the beloved apostle stated: "God is light, and in Him is no darkness at all" (1 John 1:5). James the apostle wrote: "Every good gift and every perfect gift is from above, and cometh down from the Father of lights, with whom is no variableness, neither shadow of turning." (James 1:17)

In conclusion of this chapter concerning the Son always shining, Paul the apostle, who had experienced both the darkness and the light, declared the following: "Who shall separate us from the love of Christ? Shall tribulation, or distress, or persecution, or famine, or nakedness, or peril, or sword? For I am persuaded, that neither death, nor life, nor angels, nor principalities, nor powers, nor things present, nor things to come, nor height, nor depth, nor any other creature, shall be able to separate us from the love of God, which is in Christ Jesus our Lord" (Romans 8:35,38,39).

Whether it is night, and the sun appears down, or it is during the daylight hours and clouds obscure the rays of the sun, the Son is truly always shining. What this means for you and I is that there is always hope! No matter how depressed or tormented or worthless we may feel, the Savior is ready to enfold us in the warmth and peace of His love. In fact, I believe those intense feelings of coldness and inner pain are evidence of two things: 1. His love is burning brightly for us, and 2. We are currently away from His spiritual presence.

It is part of His mercy and desire for us to feel of His love that He allows us to feel worse, the farther away we are from Him. This is His way of inviting us back to feeling closer to Him as soon as possible. Our individual spirits yearn to have the truth, and the smaller our current level of truth, the worse we feel. Deep inside, our spirits want "the truth, the whole truth, and nothing but the truth."

# PERSONAL NOTES

# PERSONAL NOTES

# Chapter 2

## Levels of Aliveness

Principle 4:  THERE ARE DIFFERENT LEVELS OF
PSYCHOLOGICAL ALIVENESS.

> *"I am the light of the world, he that followeth me shall*
> *not walk in darkness, but shall have the **light of life**."*
> St. John 8:12 (emphasis added)

Light and life are very closely interconnected.  I was reminded of
this recently.  We enjoyed receiving a large quantity of potatoes from our
friends who are farmers in our area and we asked them how long the
potatoes might store in our underground root cellar.  We were informed
that as long as we kept them in a place that was cool, dark, and dry, they
should stay firm and edible until spring.

I am writing this around Christmas time and yesterday went down
into the root cellar to get another box of potatoes and, sure enough, there
were no signs of softness or sprouting taking place.  As I placed the box of
potatoes on one of the lower shelves in a cupboard in our kitchen, I noticed
that there was still a small container in the back of the cupboard with
several potatoes.  In contrast to the ones I had just gotten from the root
cellar, these potatoes, although from the same original load, had about one-
half inch whitish sprouts.  I was impressed that the growth had occurred in
those potatoes with only the element of warmth of the house being present.
I suppose that some light had, in fact, reached them in the random opening
of the cupboard door.  I am not sure how the moisture of the air in the
house compared to the moisture content in the air of the root cellar.  Of
course, the growth of the potatoes in the house could have been even more
accelerated by increasing the amount of light and moisture. Christ, who is
"the light of the world", referred to himself as the "living waters" and
desires to enfold us in the warmth of his everlasting love.  Just like
potatoes, each of us grow spontaneously as the elements of light, water and
warmth are present.  This means that we do not grow when we allow
ourselves to stay in the darkness of depression, guilt or sin.

Christ wants us to have life more abundantly.  It is important to
realize that there are different levels of actually being alive.  These levels
of aliveness for humans to be described, vary from existing or being
dormant on the one hand, to thriving on the other.  We are meant to thrive,
and the closer we experience the source of life, the more we do thrive. (see
Diagram 3)

The commandments can be seen as gardening tips for abundant life and growth. The Master Gardener wants to teach us how to truly live and has thus commanded us to learn of Him, experience Him, and know Him: "and this is life eternal that they might know thee, the only true God and Jesus Christ whom thou has sent." (St. John 17:3)

We know others at the deepest levels when we love them. Jesus described that the greatest commandment is that, "Thou shalt love the Lord thy God with all thy heart, with all thy soul, and with all thy mind" (Matthew 22:37). An attempt will be made in this book to describe a set of principles and practical suggestions in better loving God with all our heart, mind, and soul and thereby live more abundantly.

I have personally never felt more alive than after having a beautiful, enlightening experience while preparing for my comprehensive exams in graduate school, during the spring of 1985. My plan had been to spend several months carefully reviewing my graduate studies in preparation for the week of exams, which were then two weeks away. On a Saturday morning, I went to my study area in the basement of Burnett Hall, where the psychology department was housed at the University of Nebraska-Lincoln. The advice I had been given, for studying for my exams, emphasized the need for not focusing on details, but pulling together broad themes in an overall perspective of the field of psychology and the various subspecialties in which I had been trained. As I was prayerfully going about my review, I took a brief break to relax and peacefully began to receive impressions, which led to what seemed to be a knitting together of various concepts and patterns, which I had previously not considered. It was a thrilling experience as it seemed as if everything I had ever learned in school, in my spiritual upbringing, and in my personal experience seemed to integrate into what was, for me, a massive leap in self-understanding, and in how I understood psychology and life in general. I attempted to write, outline, and otherwise capture the various thoughts as they came together.

# Diagram 3

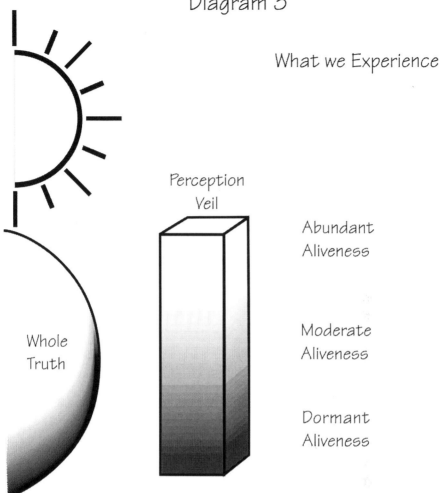

What we Experience

Perception
Veil

Whole
Truth

Abundant
Aliveness

Moderate
Aliveness

Dormant
Aliveness

"I am come that they might have life, and that they might have it more abundantly."

St. John 10:10

"He that hath the Son hath life; and he that hath not the Son of God hath not life."

1 John 5:12

For about a week following that experience, I felt extremely calm and more full of love toward others than I had ever felt. It was an intriguing time, with me, especially feeling less self conscious, something that had been difficult for me. Also remarkable, was that my senses seemed especially keen with colors appearing brighter, foods tasting better, and everything seeming more alive and delightful. I felt a oneness with nature, other people and with God, and was truly on a natural high, which Abraham Maslow called a "peak experience." I was left with no fear concerning the comprehensive exams and continued to prepare and was able to pass them (see Diagram 4).

The whole experience was beautiful and rewarding in and of itself, but was also marvelous in relation to preparing the way for me to obtain a research fellowship to conduct my doctoral dissertation. This was conducted through the funding of the Belgian-American Educational Foundation and allowed me to take my wife and children to Leuven, Belgium, where I was able to study with Dr. Willy Lens at the Research Center for Motivation and Time Perspective at the Catholic University of Leuven.

Part of the insights during my peak experience were related to how our motivational state was contributed to by how we view our personal past, present, and anticipated future. During that year in Belgium, I was introduced to the fascinating study of how time and our self concept are closely interconnected. It was a mind expanding year in many ways, with me being able to meet researchers in other specialty areas, including Guido Peeters, who was studying the area of positive-negative asymmetry. This is an interesting notion that the world is structured in a way such that the positive and negative are not symmetrical opposites, but that the positive is the more simple and basic standard, with the negative being a changed and therefore more complicated version of the standard. To state it another way, positivity would be just positivity, but negativity would **not** be just negativity, but something like "the absence of positivity". It is speculated that there is a mental bias toward positivity because positivity represents a simpler and more basic concept than negativity.

# Diagram 4

## What we Experience

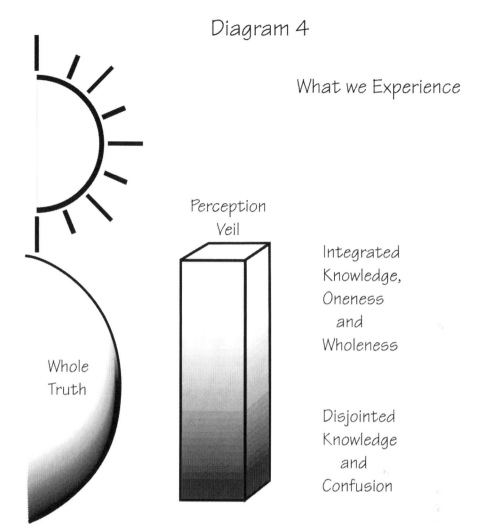

Perception
Veil

Integrated
Knowledge,
Oneness
and
Wholeness

Disjointed
Knowledge
and
Confusion

Whole
Truth

"Now the God of hope fill you with all joy and peace in believing, that ye may bound in hope through the power of the Holy Ghost. And I myself also am persuaded of you, my brethren, that ye also are full of goodness, filled with all knowledge, able also to admonish one another."

Romans 15:13

As one example of this positive-negative asymmetry, there exists many adjectives composed of a favorable root word, which is transformed into an unfavorable sense by adding a negative prefix, like "un," "in," or "dis." For example, the positive root word "true" can be changed to the less favorable "untrue," but must, in fact, have the prefix "un" added to the more simple and basic positive root word. In other words, according to the positive-negative asymmetry, it requires more effort and complexity to have negativity than to have the standard of positivity. Another example of this is the fact that more muscles are required to make a negative frown than to make a positive smile.

The dictionary defines <u>darkness</u> as the "absence of light." According to positive-negative asymmetry theory, light would be the positive standard with darkness being a state which requires effort to be less than the standard. I have learned that the word "positive" comes from a Latin root word "Positum" which means "that which is real." When I had my natural high experience, I had never felt more fully alive and real, and I had also never felt more positive. I believe that the more actually real our perceptions are, the better and more positive we feel, and the more simple things become.

It is quite easy to describe what good physical health is, in terms of various indicators such as blood pressure, heart rate, skin condition, etc. What gets complicated is attempting to describe all of the many different ways that people can be unhealthy with the myriad of diseases and disorders. In the area of mental health, there is a large manual attempting to describe the complexity of mental and emotional disorders, but the characteristics of individuals enjoying mental health are quite uniform and few in number. These include characteristics such as gratitude, patience, compassion and enjoyment of life.

Obviously, being physically healthy feels better than being physically unhealthy, just as being mentally healthy feels better than being mentally unhealthy. The healthier we are, the better we feel and the more we experience things as they really are. We could say that each of us lives in a different reality from each other, depending on how fully healthy and alive we really are. For example, Mother Teresa is living in her reality as she attempts to help others live, just as a man contemplating killing another person is living in his reality. It is important to know that not all realities are equally valid. The relative validity of our perceptions is discernable by how our reality <u>feels</u>, with the abundantly alive feelings of peace, joy and love indicating a truer and fuller reality (see Diagram 5).

# Diagram 5

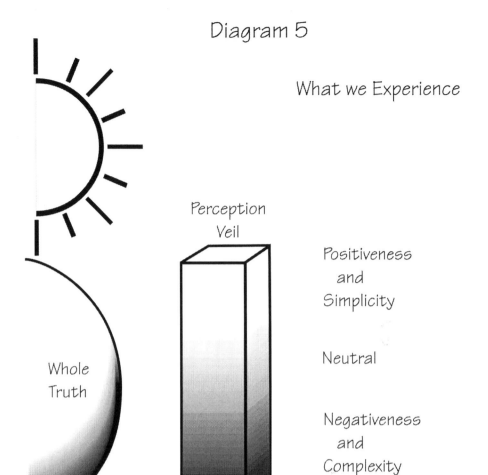

What we Experience

Perception
Veil

Positiveness
and
Simplicity

Neutral

Negativeness
and
Complexity

Whole
Truth

"Light is sown for the righteous, and gladness for the upright in heart."

Psalms 97:11

"But I fear, lest by any means, as the serpent beguiled Eve through his subtilty, so your minds should be corrupted from the simplicity that is in Christ."

2 Corinthians 11:3

In my work as a mental health professional, I have been intrigued by the fact that regardless of the problems which prompted people to seek help, a common characteristic which they all share is that their sense of self-worth has dropped. Further, the worse they feel, the lower their sense of personal worth.

There is truly nothing more real in the entire universe than the worth each of us are in the eyes of God. It is comforting to know, that the more that reality is denied by us as individuals, the more inner pain we experience (see Diagram 6).

The next section of the book will focus on how we can make our thoughts more consistent with God's thoughts, so that we can be less likely to question our worth and thereby feel better, even though we live in a world where the light and warmth are not continually experienced. It seems that the true worth of our eternal spirit is so powerful that even any slight deviation from fully recognizing that worth, is going to be made known to us by a sense of discomfort.

Our sense of worth is related to who we think we are, in comparison to who we really are. We really are children of God and each of infinite worth. That is how God always sees us, but our view of ourselves can vary. God's thoughts are higher than our thoughts, and the next portion of the book is an attempt to help us understand how we can more fully love God with all our hearts, and thereby have our thoughts more fully match God's thoughts about His children. To the extent our thoughts match His thoughts, the better we feel.

# Diagram 6

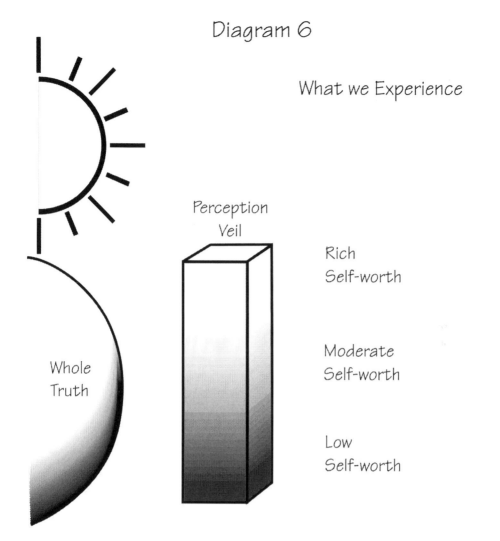

What we Experience

Perception
Veil

Rich
Self-worth

Moderate
Self-worth

Low
Self-worth

Whole
Truth

"For my thoughts are not your thoughts, neither are your ways my ways, saith the Lord.  For as the heavens are higher than the earth, so are my ways higher than your ways, and my thoughts than your thoughts."

Isaiah 55: 8,9

You are most alive
when
Christ is alive in you.

author unknown

# PERSONAL NOTES

# SECTION II

## Loving God with all Your Heart

# Chapter 3

## Seeing Through Moods

Principle #5  WE ALL HAVE MOOD CHANGES.  WHEN OUR MOOD GOES DOWN, OUR SPIRITUAL HEART GROWS SMALLER AND OUR LIGHT AND WISDOM  DECREASES, USUALLY WITHOUT US BEING AWARE OF THE CHANGE
INITIALLY.

*"But became vain in their imaginations, and their foolish heart was darkened.*
*Professing themselves to be wise, they became fools."*
(Romans 1:21,22)

The actions of the heart and mind are both interconnected.  When our "spirits are up" we are light-hearted, and when our "spirits are down" we are down-hearted or heavy-hearted.  It is very important to know that as our spirits drop and our mood goes down, our thinking quality also goes down.  It is as if when things become darker, a dimmer switch is being turned down, diminishing the light and the spiritual intelligence.  This is why we say and do "dumb" things when we are in a low mood--because we actually are dumber at those times.

When a person is severely depressed, there are noticeable drops in intellectual functioning as measured by formal intelligence tests.  For example, when I was on my clinical internship at the V.A. Medical Center in Tucson, Arizona, one of my training rotations was on the geriatric unit.  Several times it was emphasized to the psychology interns that we must be very careful so as to not diagnose an elderly person as having dementia (biologically reduced brain functioning) when they may actually be appearing severely reduced in mental functioning due to clinical depression.  Even when lower moods are less severe than clinical depression, we experience diminished thinking quality.  The trouble is, we become too dumb to know we are dumb.  In other words, a tremendously important mental trap to be aware of is that we almost always assume that our thinking is of equal quality at all times.  It is vitally important to understand that our thinking quality can vary dramatically (see Diagram 7).

Wouldn't it be nice if we were able to tell when our own thinking quality or the thinking quality of another person was diminished.  Then we would be able to better assess how much weight or validity to give the thoughts.  Or in other words, we would better know how seriously we ought to take certain thoughts.

I would like to describe three handy indicators of when our thinking quality is low so that we can better assess the quality of our thoughts and thus better know how to act accordingly. The first to be discussed will be an internal sense of pressure which increases as our mood goes down; the second being the fact that our thoughts become "stickier" and harder to dismiss as our mood goes down; and the third being that we take everything more personally as our mood goes down.

### Pressure: Our Internal Barometer

Perhaps you have attempted to push a basketball or some other inflatable object under water. If you are careful, you can get it below the surface, and then if you stay right on top of it, you can keep it down, even though it is as if it fights to get back to the surface. The further down you push the basketball, the more pressure you feel against your hand and the more the basketball squirms. If you lose your grip, or otherwise stop fighting the pressure, the basketball will shoot out of the water and settle back on top, where it is in equilibrium again.

Our spirits always want to be on top and not held down. I like to view internal emotional pressure as a helpful signal that we have dropped below our natural element where the spirit can more fully breathe. The higher the sense of internal pressure, the lower our thought quality, the more narrow our perspective, and the more likely we are to get into trouble, if we act on the pressure filled low quality thoughts. This is vitally important to know, because without this understanding, a low quality thought becomes blown out of proportion by agitation from the internal pressure. When a mercury barometer drops, it indicates a storm is coming. Inside of us, when our mood drops, the increasing pressure can signal us that a storm is coming, if we pay too much attention to the lower quality thought, which naturally occurs when pressure is high.

When you have
a sinking feeling,
head for
higher ground.


Ryan Hulbert

# Diagram 7

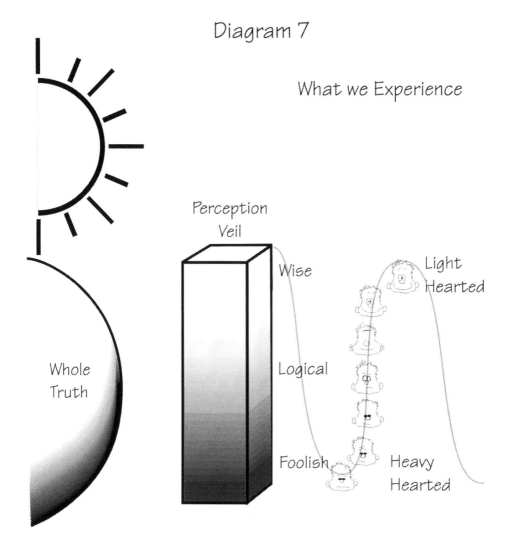

What we Experience

Perception Veil

Wise

Light Hearted

Whole Truth

Logical

Foolish

Heavy Hearted

"Wisdom is before him that hath understanding; but the eyes of a fool are in the ends of the earth."

Proverbs 17:24

"For as a man thinketh in his heart, so is he."

Proverbs 23:7

(Changes in the level of the mood or heart changes the thinking quality of the person)

Not only is it very important to recognize that our own thinking becomes impaired when pressure is high, it is important to recognize that the thinking of others also follows the same pattern. When receiving training from Dr. Bill Petitt, M.D., a psychiatrist at the Cherokee Mental Health Institute, he encouraged us when we saw another person under pressure and obviously agitated, to picture on their forehead blinking lights signaling "OUT TO LUNCH--OUT TO LUNCH--OUT TO LUNCH." Dr. Petitt also said that attempting to talk to someone in such a state of mind was pointless and said, "In such a state of mind, a person's ears retract into their head. It looks like the ears are there, but it is just a hologram!" Unfortunately, without knowing any better, we often attempt to solve our problems while in a low mood, when everything is pressurized and has an agitated sense of urgency. If two people are both interacting from a low state of mind, the likelihood of successfully communicating and problem solving is extremely low.

Probably one of the most helpful statements I have heard in years, which has been attributed to Albert Einstein, is the following: "Problems are never solved on the level at which they were created". There are solutions and growth enhancing answers to life's problems, but in fact, they are often not visible during times of lower mood.

A very important trap to be aware of is that Satan, the father of darkness, would like to keep us in the dark through having us attempt to solve our problems while in a low mood. I have heard it said that he has two major strategies to get us to feel miserable. The first and most direct strategy is an attempt to "convince us." He tries to convince us to do unhealthy and harmful things which then lead to heartache and misery. If he cannot convince us, he uses strategy number two: "confuse us." One of the chief ways he attempts to confuse us is through having us extend much energy, time and determination, in trying to solve a problem by looking for a solution in an area where the solution can never be found (see Diagram 8). Solutions become more evident as there is increased light, greater clarity and increased perspective.

# Diagram 8

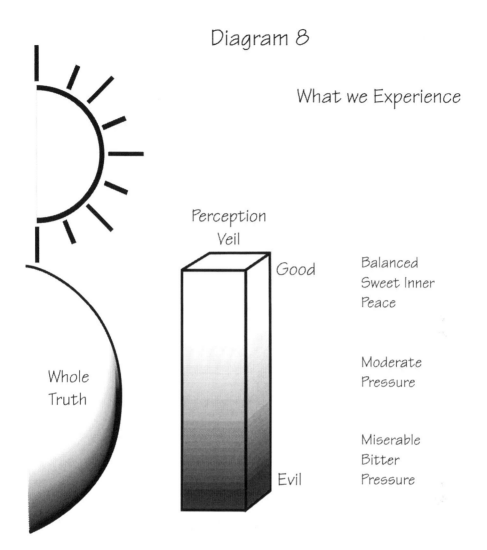

What we Experience

Perception
Veil

Whole
Truth

Good

Evil

Balanced
Sweet Inner
Peace

Moderate
Pressure

Miserable
Bitter
Pressure

"Woe unto them that call evil good, and good evil; that put darkness for light, and light for darkness; that put bitter for sweet and sweet for bitter."

Isaiah 5:20

Problems are never
solved on the
level at which
they were
created.


Albert Einstein

## Sticky Cockle Burr Thoughts

In addition to internal pressure, a second helpful indicator that our moods are lower and our thinking quality reduced, is the relative "stickiness" of our thoughts. By "sticky," I mean the characteristic of our thoughts when we have only one irritating topic on our mind that we cannot seem to get rid of. Have you ever had a cockle burr or some other type of irritating weed attached to your clothing, your hair, or in a pet's fur? This is analogous to having an irritating or otherwise unhealthy thought stuck in your mind that you have difficulty shaking loose.

This is a helpful signal that your thought quality is reduced and that you are lower than you might have been aware. Consider the whole world and even the universe of things to think about. When in a low state of mind, we do not have the freedom to selectively move about among the various topics, but rather feel locked on to a very narrow realm of contents or themes. Thank goodness such a state of mind feels bad so we know that we are not seeing the broader picture (see Diagram 9).

I have a brief object lesson that I like to share with clients to help them better read the signal of when their thoughts are sticky and narrow. On the wall of my office is a picture and I invite clients to stand several feet from the picture and relax their mind so that they can see the whole picture with their peripheral vision. I then ask them to look through a "sophisticated device," which is actually just a toilet paper tube. By closing one eye and looking through the tube, they report now not being able to see the whole picture. I explain to them that in order to solve our problems, our spirit wants to see the whole picture. It attempts to let us know when we are not seeing the whole picture, by constricting sensations. Such a pinched and tight feeling can let us know that although with our physical eyes our peripheral vision usually seems equally broad, our spiritual vision, with its accompanying wisdom and inspiration, is temporarily reduced.

I find it interesting that my clients, upon putting the tube to their eye, have a tendency to take a step back in order to not have such a constricted view. By taking only about three or four steps back, they are able to see the whole picture, even with continuing to look through the tube. When in a pinched frame of mind, we would do well to not step forward in behaving, but to metaphorically step back several paces in order to get some space to better assess our situation and options.

# Diagram 9

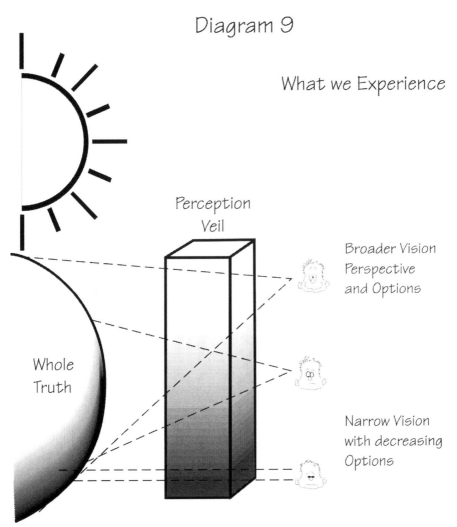

What we Experience

Perception Veil

Broader Vision Perspective and Options

Whole Truth

Narrow Vision with decreasing Options

"To open their eyes, and to turn them from darkness to light, and from the power of Satan unto God."

Acts 26:18

(Satan can confuse good-hearted, well-intentioned persons by having them spend all their energies looking for solutions where they cannot be found.)

In contrast to stepping back, is the unhealthy tendency we have to try to solve our problems while in a pinched state of mind. To help clients understand the futility of such attempts, I ask them to compare the three-inch tube to several minutes of focusing on a problem while in a pinched state of mind. While they continue looking through the tube, I tell them that I'm going to symbolically have them experience what happens to our vision when we continue spending several more minutes in the same state of mind. While doing this, I hold up another cardboard tube and place it on the end of the tube they are looking through. Their reaction is often quite impressive when they experience the portion of the visible picture, now becoming dramatically more constricted. Thank goodness the longer we focus on something in a constricted state of mind, the tighter it feels, which is an attempt to signal us of the unhealthy nature of our mental effort.

<u>Increased Self Consciousness</u>

To this point we have discussed the low quality thinking indicators of pressure and narrow and sticky thoughts. The next indicator, one which has been especially helpful for me personally in determining my thought quality at any given time, is the fact that as our mood and thought quality go down, our self consciousness increases. In such sates of mind, we become more and more self-absorbed and begin taking everything personally. In a healthier state of mind, on the other hand, we tend to not take things personally and are less affected by negative comments or behaviors.

When healthy, we are more involved in observing our surroundings and other people, and experiencing things as interesting and pleasant. When self-absorbed, our connections to the outside world seem to diminish while we turn our focus inward and painfully begin questioning our adequacy and worth.

To illustrate this point, picture a tall building that has an elevator on the outside of the building which is made of glass, which is allowing people to watch their surroundings while they are going up and down in the elevator. Let's imagine that we are in the elevator on the top floor, and are looking through the window-like doors at the interesting scenery. In the elevator of our mind, as the elevator goes down, away from the healthy upper floors, let's imagine that more and more dark pigment is progressively added to the glass elevator doors the further down the elevator goes. Because of the dark pigment on the outside of the windows, as we go down we begin to experience the doors less like windows and more like mirrors, with us seeing our own reflection, rather than the interesting scenery on the other side of the doors. Whenever you experience a painful mood drop following someone's comment or behavior, it is similar to a mirror suddenly appearing and reflecting on you. That can be a signal that your mood has dropped and that your thinking quality at that instant may be lower than you were aware.

As another example of this phenomenon, when I go into my office early in the morning and turn on the light, I can comb my hair in the window, because with the darkness outside, it serves as a mirror. As the sun rises, and the darkness fades, my image also fades, and the window no longer serves as a mirror, but serves its purpose of allowing me to see what is going on outside. It is interesting that the mirror effect only occurs when I turn the light on in the inside of the room. I like to think of this as symbolic of the fact that the Light of Christ can come through us, to at least a certain extent, even when we are in a low mood. When the light reflects off of darkness, meaning being in a lower mood level, we receive feedback from the relative degree of spiritual darkness according to how prominent the painful self-reflection (see Diagram 10).

For example, in a moderate mood level, there may be some degree of self-focus, whereas in a lower mood level, self-focus is more intense. This more intense self-focus is not an indicator that our worth has diminished (something that is impossible), but is an indicator of our mood level and the associated quality of our thoughts. That is why in a clear and healthy state of mind, when our mood is bright, we are not self conscious but are at ease and gratefully observing and participating with the world around us.

# Diagram 10

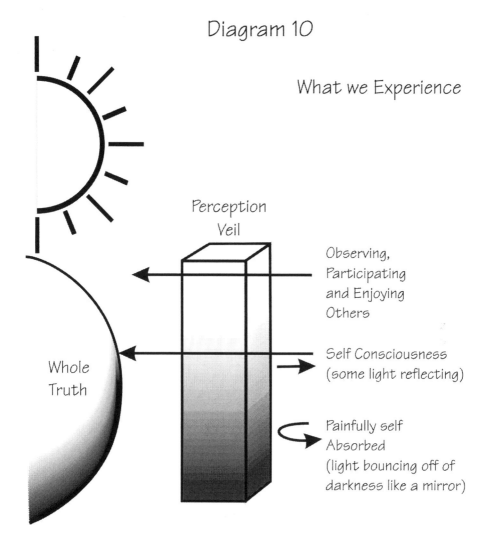

What we Experience

Perception Veil

Observing, Participating and Enjoying Others

Self Consciousness (some light reflecting)

Whole Truth

Painfully self Absorbed (light bouncing off of darkness like a mirror)

"They meet with darkness in the daytime, and grope in the noonday as in the night."

Job 5:14

A small trouble is like a pebble.
Hold it close to your eye,
and it puts everything out of focus.
Hold it at proper viewing distance,
and it can be examined and classified.
Throw it at your feet,
And it can be seen in its true setting,
just one more tiny bump on the
pathway to eternity.

Celia Luce

## Biological Influences on Mood Cycles

It is important to know that the general low mood indicators previously discussed in this chapter, along with more individual indicators, occur on a regular basis due to even subtle changes influenced by our mortal body. Once we are aware that biological changes influence our mood and thinking quality, we are better able to discriminate times when we are thinking more accurately, and thus are better able to behave accordingly. Each of the biological factors to be discussed can separately influence our mood, but also various combinations of these can occur which result in even more powerful influences on our mood.

## Time of Day Mood Influences

Currently being on a temporal earth, our bodies are tied to the rhythms of the earth and its light and dark cycles. These are referred to as circadian rhythms, or the diurnal cycle. I am a "morning person" for example, and am clearest and most alive before noon and in the early afternoon. In the past, I had a predictable experience around 9 p.m. each night, when a heavy fatigue washed over me, my mood lowered and everything suddenly looked different -- my children were less interesting and little things about the house not being tidy began to grow like monsters before my eyes. Everything became urgent, such as the children needing to brush their teeth this very minute! Now that I am a little older, that wave of fatigue starts even earlier, at about 8:30 p.m. One major difference about me, however, is that I am learning to comprehend the level of my mood and am less inclined to buy into the urgent low mood thoughts, and am learning to keep my "profound" comments to myself at that time.

Another vulnerable time of day for me is around 2 p.m., especially if my lunch included heavier foods or too much food. At those times, my head starts to swim and basically any task I am doing seems burdensome. Obviously, those times of day which are vulnerable for us, as individuals, are not the times to be making important decisions or comments. This might have been what Solomon had in mind when he said, "A fool uttereth all his mind; but a wise man keepeth it in till afterwards." (Proverbs 29:11) Not everything that enters our minds at any given time, is worth sharing with others.

37

Blood Sugar Influences on Mood

Between meals, even before our stomach rumbles and we are aware we are hungry, our blood sugar has started to drop with a corresponding drop in our mood and thinking quality. In such a state of mind, we are ripe for grumpiness. Children especially, with their high rate of metabolism, need frequent nourishment, and without it become more irritable. Some of the toughest times in our home are right before supper. The meal preparation usually takes longer than we had wanted, and without knowing why, family members are more scattered in their thinking and more irritable. Even just a few bites into the meal, the mood begins to change, probably, in large measure, due to the fact that people's mouths are full and no longer vocalizing their relatively irritated state of mind. As the blood sugar kicks in, the conversation can turn to more pleasant things.

Little children, especially, need frequent snacks and other nourishment or they tend to get agitated and begin to focus on negative things. Dr. Pettit told of the humorous example of his young daughter getting in a low mood and systematically pointing out all of the things about her life she didn't like. As her list grew, her frustration mounted until she finally exclaimed, "And why did we paint this house yellow!"

In addition to the general need of blood sugar from regular and healthy nourishment, the issue of blood sugar regulation is very important for people who have diabetes. Dramatic fluctuations in mental clarity and thinking ability occur when blood sugar levels for people with diabetes have not been carefully monitored. Again, it is very important to know the small and early warning signs of the beginning of such fluctuations, to intervene as early as possible before the mental state is changed to the point of being in danger of health problems, but no longer thinking clearly enough to know that one is in danger.

I once heard about a smart mother who met her children at the door as they came from school. Knowing their blood sugar--and their moods-- were probably a little out of balance, she gave each child a spoonful of peanut butter and sent them to their room for 15 minutes or until their bodies and moods had mellowed out a bit.

Here's the point we all need to remember. Our physical body needs regular and healthy nourishment; without it, the body, mind and spirit cannot work well together.

There is a film which encourages recovering alcoholics to use the memory device "HALT." This stands for not letting themselves get too HUNGRY, ANGRY, LONELY, or TIRED. Any of those situations make them more vulnerable to less quality thoughts and thus more susceptible to the temptation of relapsing into the use of alcohol or other drugs. Such low quality thoughts are often referred to as "stinking thinking."

## Hormones and Mood Fluctuations

Both men and women have hormonal fluctuations, with women, usually having it more pronounced because of the menstrual cycle. Women, of course, vary in terms of how much their moods are affected by changes in their hormonal cycle, with some of them being quite strongly influenced. When more aware of what is happening and especially with the early signs of such changes occurring, people can be better equipped to modify both their expectations and the amount of weight they should give to their thoughts during such periods of time. I have heard some women who have strong hormonal reactions openly warning people around them through statements such as, "Don't listen to a thing I say for the next five days!"

---

**HALT!**

Don't let yourself get
Too

**H**ungry
**A**ngry
**L**onely
**T**ired

---

Understanding the influence of hormonal changes is very important in interacting productively with teenagers. Teenagers are not only going through dramatic hormonal changes, but are also going through such changes for the first time. No wonder it can be confusing for both teenagers and their parents.

In this discussion of hormones, comes the issue of menopausal changes and also changes which may occur in someone's glandular system, such as the thyroid. The main point of this section is to highlight how our bodily functioning, in relation to hormones, can greatly effect our mood levels and thinking quality, and to thus be better aware of what is going on and behave in the most productive ways possible.

A heartbreaking example of making a decision while having ones thinking quality influenced by hormones, was told by a client of mine while living in the midwest. This young father came to me distraught, following attempting to deal with the depression and confusion related to his wife leaving him. He reported that they had had a number of years of happy marriage and had several children. One day, upon coming home from work, he found that she had packed the car and was getting the children ready to drive halfway across the country to where her parents lived, because she was leaving him. As he attempted to find out what was wrong, she could give him no clear explanations, but simply stated that for several days she had felt very unhappy in the marriage and felt like her only solution was to leave him. As she walked out the door, she said, almost as an afterthought, "You know the strange thing is, this whole thing could be nothing but hormones." Unfortunately she did leave, and according to him, she had apparently given a number of reasons to her family members, which he viewed as her after having made the decision, now attempting to justify her actions.

Just like with the woman in the above story, often when our thinking is distorted due to bodily influences, there is a sense of confusion and questioning we have of things not seeming quite right. As we are better able to pick up subtle cues of diminished thinking quality, we are less likely to be trapped by such low states of mind, even though they at times are very convincing.

## Alcohol and Other Drug Influences on Mood

The active ingredient in alcohol, ethanol, is a central nervous system depressant. Even with relatively small amounts of ethanol, our thinking quality is affected. At relatively low levels of blood alcohol, people can be aware that they are becoming intoxicated, but at higher levels of blood alcohol, individuals become too drunk to know they are drunk. The scary thing is that even though their thinking is very impaired, they are not aware that it is impaired, and are likely to attempt to drive a vehicle or do other things that they assume they are able to do at a normal level of performance.

For much of my career as a mental health professional, I have worked with chemically dependent clients. Periodically through the years, a person has called me who has relapsed and was attempting to communicate with me over the phone, while in a drunken state. After this happened a number of times, I noticed that a common feature of their communication style was repeating themselves over and over again. I was curious about this and finally was able to talk with a client about such a conversation several days later, when the person was sober. I asked the person if he could tell me why he had gone over the same thing many times, even after I had conveyed to him that I understood. He appeared somewhat embarrassed and said he had repeated himself because what he was trying to tell me seemed so important at that time that he wanted to make sure that I hadn't missed it. I can assure you that what he had been talking about was not profound, but in his drunken state he apparently thought that it was.

## Lunar Influences on Mood

Much research and speculation has been done on the gravitational pull of the moon, as it relates to changes in biological and behavioral functioning. As you know, the gravitational pull of the moon is what influences the ocean tides. I have heard it said that we as humans are at least 60 percent liquid, and it stands to reason that if the tides of the ocean are influenced by the pull of the moon, that we and other life forms could experience some gravitational tugs also. Very few people I have met have indicated being influenced to the point of feeling a noticeable difference in their mood or sense of well being when the moon is full. Some, however, have reported feeling a noticeable difference, and a number who work in institutions, such as restaurants or hospitals, have reported general patterns of differences in their clientele, in terms of increased agitation.

41

There are certainly other biological influences on moods which affect our thinking quality, but the purpose of this section is to simply highlight several common bodily factors to have us become more sensitive to possible reasons why we are, at times, feeling low for no apparent reason.

Once after discussing some of these factors with a group, a business woman came up to me afterwards and gave an interesting example of experiencing some of these factors. She had been waiting for about half an hour for a male supervisee for a business luncheon appointment at a restaurant. She became more and more irritated with his lateness and began making a list of the things she wanted to discuss with him about his job performance. As the list grew, it began including very specific items about his behavior she felt needed correcting. Finally when he came, the meal was fairly rushed and did not allow for her to discuss the things on her list. The next day in the office, she wanted to hold the discussion with the supervisee, that she had not been able to hold over lunch the previous day. As she reviewed her list created while she was hungry and angry, now being in a different state of mind, she could not believe how knit-picky and off-base almost all of her comments were, and wisely chose not to use that list as a basis for their discussion (see Diagram 11).

## GRACEFULLY DOWN

Following hearing some of these thoughts at an alumni meeting for people who had gone through a recovery program for chemical dependency, a woman raised her hand and asked an important question. She said in a suspicious tone, "Do you mean to say that if I follow some of these principles, that I won't ever feel down?" I complimented her and her question and said, "No. That's a very important point that I am glad to attempt to clarify. What I am saying is that when you understand these things, you can better recognize when you are down and then, when you, in fact, realize that you are down, put less weight on the accuracy of your thoughts at that point.

42

# Diagram 11

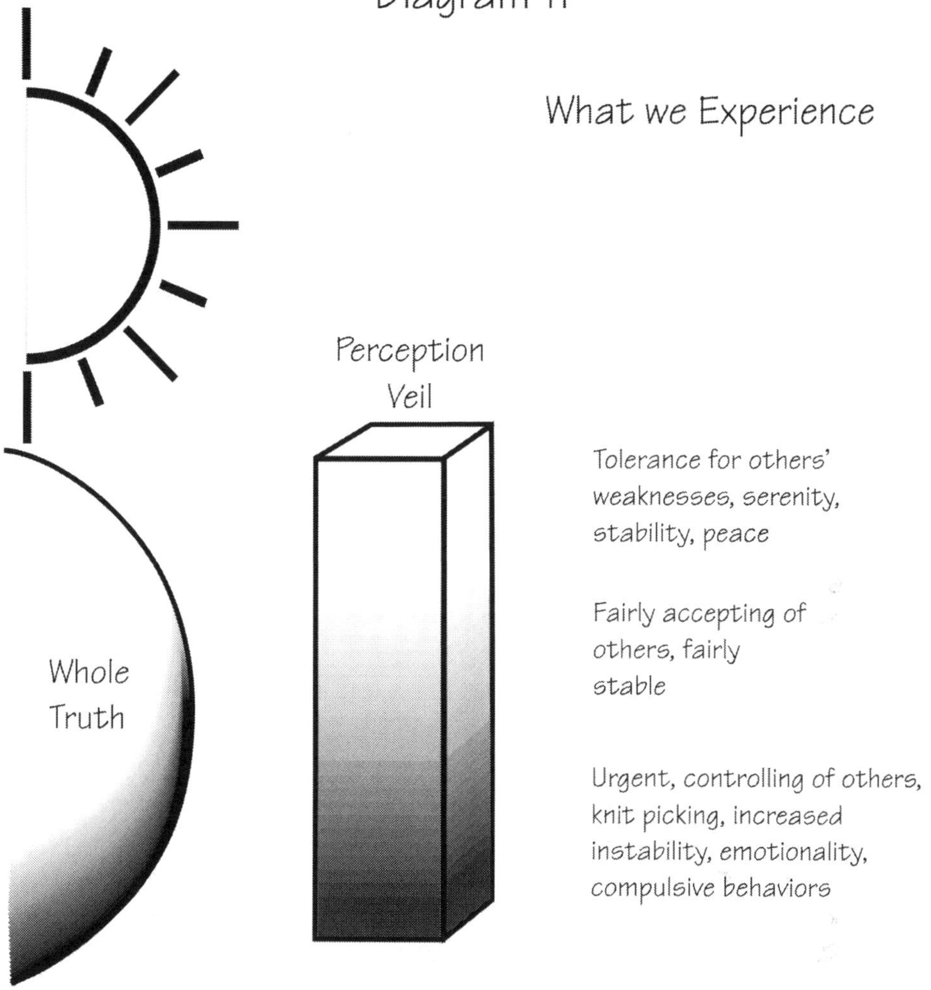

## What we Experience

Perception
Veil

Whole
Truth

Tolerance for others'
weaknesses, serenity,
stability, peace

Fairly accepting of
others, fairly
stable

Urgent, controlling of others,
knit picking, increased
instability, emotionality,
compulsive behaviors

But if ye have bitter envying and strife in your hearts, glory not, and lie not against the truth. This wisdom descendeth not from above, but is earthly, sensual, devilish. For where envying and strife is, there is confusion and every evil work. But the wisdom that is from above is first pure; then peaceable, gentle, and easy to be intreated, full of mercy and good fruits, without partiality, and without hypocrisy."

James 3:14-17

Then you could be more gracefully down!" With that explanation, she laughed and went on to explain briefly that she was the manager of an office and thought of getting buttons for each her office workers to pull out when they were feeling vulnerable. They could thereby warn their colleagues to not take them so seriously by the button with the words "GRACEFULLY DOWN" (see Diagram 12).

When discussing this notion with a male client, we talked about how it would be nice if we had a sort of "mental dipstick" to assess our mood at any given time and thereby know how much weight to put on our relative thought quality at that moment. He chuckled and said, "Yeah, then you could tell if you were a quart low or not!" We chuckled together and then he went on to explain how he had heard on a radio program how in some Japanese settings, people had worn color-coded buttons. These colors represented a well understood continuum of well being, and were a symbol to communicate to others how much to expect of them at the time. A button with a color representing a relatively low state of well being would be a handy way of, in essence, telling others, "I'm not feeling the best today. Please give me a break and not expect too much."

It is important to know about and accept the fact that people in general, and each of us in particular, at times, have dark moods. The changes in our moods may be less obvious than the earth rotating away from the sun as night falls, but they are none the less just as real. When we understand that the darkness of night is related to the earth's rotation, we then also understand and expect that the night will not last forever. The famous psychiatrist, Carl Jung, encouraged people to recognize that each of us have a "dark side," so that we do not deny it, but also learn to not act out of the influences of the dark side.

Our normal, or in other words, that which we are accustomed to, is often quite different from that which is healthy. It is interesting, however, that even though it might be mildly uncomfortable at times, we often don't know how uncomfortable it is, until we have experienced increases in our health.

# Diagram 12

Gracefully Down:
Being aware you are in a lower mood
and not acting on the limited perceptions
and impaired thinking.

Perception
Veil

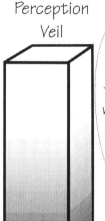

I'm really feeling low, but I have come to realize that my perceptions are not trustworthy when I feel this way. I'm not going to believe or act on what I'm thinking. I'll go easy on myself and others instead, and have hope to come out of this.

Whole
Truth

"When his candle shined upon my head, and when by his light I walked through darkness."

Job 29:3

"When I fall, I shall arise; when I sit in darkness, the Lord shall be a light unto me."

Micah 7:8

"Wherein ye greatly rejoice, though now for a season, if need be, ye are in heaviness through manifold temptations.

1 Peter 1:6

My wife has a very difficult time getting me to go shopping. During the buying of my most recent pair of dress shoes, I had a very interesting experience in relation to sensing the difference between normal and healthy. I'd had my good old shoes for several years; and, although they had become quite worn, they were still very comfortable to me and I felt that they still had a lot of good wear on them. My wife convinced me to, at least, try on a new pair of shoes. As I slipped them on and took a few steps, I was truly amazed at the real comfort I was experiencing. Immediately, the level of comfort in my old shoes paled in comparison. I had to try on my old pair again just to see if that new level of comfort was just in my imagination. It wasn't, and I gladly gave my old shoes to my oldest boy who thought they felt really great!

As we sample more and more of our natural state of health, our "normal" becomes more and more uncomfortable as we have appreciation of the true worth each of us have a right to feel as children of God.

How can anyone see straight
when he does not even see himself
and that darkness which he himself
carries unconsciously into
all his dealings?

Carl Jung

# Mood Related Memories

Principle #6  MEMORIES HAVE AN EMOTIONAL TONE TO THEM TO TELL US HOW MUCH IN HARMONY THE MEMORY IS WITH OUR TRUE WORTH.

*"What God hath cleaned that call not thou common."*
Acts 10:15
*"Happy is the man that findeth wisdom, and the man that getteth understanding."*
Proverbs 3:13

In 1993, while working at the Cherokee Mental Health Institute in Cherokee, Iowa, I had the fortunate opportunity of interacting for several months with Tom Lucas, a semi-retired psychiatrist from Lincoln, Nebraska.  One of our hospital's psychiatrists was away for several months, and Dr. Lucas had been hired to help us in the interim.  I became intrigued with his wisdom, sense of humor, and kindliness, and took several opportunities to visit with him personally and discuss aspects of psychotherapeutic healing.

During one especially meaningful discussion for me, he described his view of how all therapies were ultimately helpful through changing a person's feelings.  He elaborated that whether the techniques included more of an emphasis on thinking or behavior or any other general style, significant change in the person only took place once feelings were changed.

He then asked me why I thought change in feelings must take place before a real shift in a person's overall approach to living life more healthily could occur.  I told him that I was not sure, and he went on to explain a fascinating view.  In the center of our brain is a collection of small nuclei, which together form what is called the limbic system.  The limbic system performs many important functions, including the regulation of feelings and emotions.  Dr. Lucas explained that each of our five senses which bring input from the outside world connect first through nerve pathways to the limbic system.  Thus, information from our sight, smell, taste, hearing, and touch first goes through the limbic system and, in turn, then goes to the wrinkly, outer covering of the brain, which is call the cortex.

I began to see the profound implications of what he was explaining as he pointed out that our memories stored in the cortex are thus not objective "snapshots" of what we experience through our senses, but are, in fact, "mood-related memories" based on the prevailing feeling state of the limbic system at the time these sensory inputs were experienced. In other words, we can think of a memory as being "color coded," through which the sensory input passes on its way to being encoded in the cortex.

As an example of this, people feel sentimental about certain old songs because the limbic system encoded their memory of the song with the feelings they experienced with the music. For example, a friend of mine said that every time he hears "Blue Velvet," he remembers dancing with a high school girlfriend at the junior-senior prom.

The same thing happens to car buffs when they see a beautifully restored '56 Chevy. They not only remember the car, but they experience all over again the feelings they felt when they used to hang out at the drive-in, where everyone ogled at them and their cool '56 Chevy. The limbic system is what makes our memory different from computer memory.

I would like to further elaborate on the concept of mood related memories in the form of an analogy. Let's imagine the individual memories as each being a file card with information on them, each of which have a color coded tag. Thus, if two people observed a certain event, and if those two people were on a different mood level, they may have a file card registered in their memory with quite similar information, but a dissimilar color code. Due to the different mood state and corresponding color coding, one memory would be recalled with greater or lesser degrees of pleasantness, depending on the mood of the person when the experience occurred.

Let's compare our memories to a library of information. Picture a seven story library which has its materials categorized, not by the content such as history or geology, but by the color coding of the memories. For example, on the top floor would be all of the materials with a bright color coding and materials on the other floors would, floor by floor away from the top floor, have gradually decreasing brightness to the point of darkness. This library has a unique elevator which only wants to go up. It takes effort to have it go to the lower floors and when left to its own devices, is anti-qravity in terms of moving toward the top floors.

In our imagination, let's now transform those color coded file cards to books, with each memory being represented by a single book. In the library are thousands and millions of individual books distributed among the floors, according to the mood of the person when the books were "written". Imagine looking at such a library of an individual who had a traumatic and often very tense childhood. As children, we are wonderful sensing devices, taking everything about life in as quickly as we can. We use all of our senses as if we are hungry for information and can not get enough of life through tasting it, watching it, smelling it, hearing it, and touching it. Thus, in childhood, volumes are stacked in the library at a tremendous rate. As we grow older, unfortunately, our intrigue with life in general often tends to wane, with us not using our senses nearly so often, with the resulting slowing down of adding new books to our library.

A person who had a majority of books in their library stored as a child on lower mood floors, would hopefully have quite a few books also stored on, at least, the moderate mood level floors and also, a few in the higher mood level floors. Interestingly, it appears that although the elevator always wants to go up, it tends to sag down in the library according to the center of gravity corresponding to the location of the majority of the books.

One client with whom I was discussing this, gave the helpful comparison of these books to magnets. Each book is like a magnet and the metal elevator would be pulled toward the floor or floors with the majority of the magnets. The elevator represents where each of us are individually on the mood levels at a particular time. We can literally be in only one physical location at a time, and where we are at mood-wise at any given time, influences the perceptions we have of the world, and also the memories we have more available in our mind.

Depending on which floor we currently are, the memories of that floor seem to be most available and subsequently "real" to us, while memories on the other floors have more of a sense of vagueness to the point of us, at times, even questioning whether those memories actually took place. Upon moving to another floor, those particular memories gain more in realness and availability to us. For example, I have a particular gray mood memory of dropping the baton in the last race as a senior in high school, in the state track meet in the mile relay. Thank goodness, I was able to pick it up quickly and my team was able to still do fairly well in the race. Nevertheless, that is a gray memory for me. I almost never think of that experience, and have done so only several times following about a year after it happened. Interestingly, the times when I did recall that experience, were when I was feeling low from being especially tired and stressed. It was as if I had gone to that floor where among other gray memories, that particular gray memory was stored.

When you are inside of a building in an elevator, it is hard to know exactly what floor you are on. To help in knowing your location, elevators have floor indicators by having a light come on to show which floor you are either on or approaching. Also, to let you know when you have arrived on a floor where the doors will be opening, a small chime or tone is heard. In all elevators I have ever been in, that tone remains the same, regardless of the floor number. In this elevator analogy we are currently describing, in the mood-related memory library of our mind, the tone varies according

51

to the various floors. For example, the tone has a pleasant and soft sound in the upper floors, where our pleasant experiences are stored, with that tone changing to be less pleasant and more rumbly or bass-like as the elevator goes down. On the lowest floors, the tone is loud and is more like a deep GONG sound, which resonates through your whole body.

These tones could be comparable to our feelings, which are there to either invite us or to warn us according to the relative helpfulness of the data on any given floor. It is believed that literally everything we experience is stored in our minds, both the good and the bad. Not all of what we have experienced is helpful for us to dwell on (see Diagram 13).

The realness of a memory grows according to whether or not we are on a similar mood level as when the memory was formed. If we begin to dwell on a lower mood memory, our elevator begins to descend to that floor, which in turn begins to bring that memory back to life. The negative vibrations which occur when the elevator arrives at that floor could serve as a warning to the unhelpfulness of that data in our current life. If we were not aware of the warning nature of the unpleasant feeling tone, upon opening the doors on that floor, we can become trapped by the fact that the negative vibrations actually do begin to have the memory be less of a memory and more of a reliving of that experience.

Another client, in discussing this concept, said that it is as if when we dissect a memory, it comes back to life. This can be comparable to an audio-visual center on each of the floors of the library. Focusing on a memory on a given floor causes it to grow in intensity and vividness, such as first listening to a memory on an audio tape, then watching it on a black and white video tape, then a color video tape, progressing to watching it on a big screen, then in 3-D, and finally having the perception that it is actually happening again and you are reliving the situation.

This understanding has profound implications for us in terms of our overall feeling of well-being, our problem solving, and our relationships. Whatever we focus on, at whatever mood level, becomes more and more real to us. Because people can often be on different mood levels and thus have different viewpoints, all of us could easily be trapped in our own separate "worlds." There is another essential element to help guide us to assess the larger reality at any given time and how helpful particular memories are. This important standard by which all of our mood related memories can be evaluated is our feeling tone. Thank goodness that however real and vivid a painful memory is experienced, the painful nature of the memory is an indication of how unhelpful that memory is to us in the present. Our spirit is a present-oriented being that only wants the freshest, most valid, information to help us solve our problems and find joy.

If your belief in your worth
is too low,
you will often get headaches
from bumping your head
against your artificial ceiling.

Ryan Hulbert

# Diagram 13

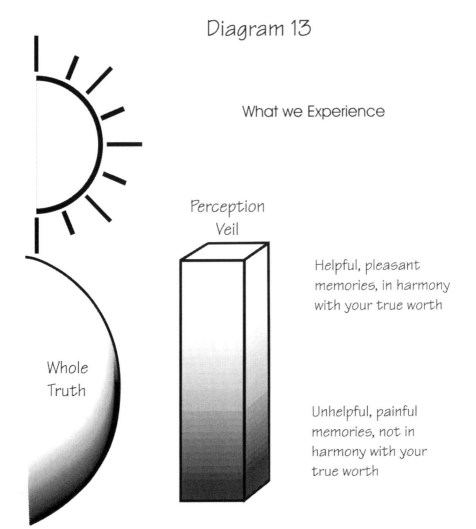

What we Experience

Perception
Veil

Helpful, pleasant
memories, in harmony
with your true worth

Whole
Truth

Unhelpful, painful
memories, not in
harmony with your
true worth

"Set your affection on things above, not on things on the earth."
Colossians 3:2

"For where your treasure is, there shall your heart be also."
St. Matthew 6:21

(For where your heart level is, there shall the quality of your memories be also.)

.        Let's examine this regarding a troubled relationship.  Yes, painful events have occurred and, yes, those are still stored on the mood floor where they occurred.  Their relative helpfulness to the current situation is the big question.  Yes, focusing on past painful experiences bring them to life and color our sense of hopefulness in interacting in the relationship, <u>but</u> whether or not those memories are helpful to us will be communicated to us by our spirit according to the feeling tone, whether pleasant or discomforting.

In doing a research paper, we would be unwise to not look for the freshest possible research, and to be careful in assessing its quality and validity.  What if we ignore new data and use musty old findings, which have either been disproven or simply support our own bias?  Quality data, just like quality experiences in a relationship from the past, is more valid than unquality data, no matter how much of that unquality data has been collected and analyzed.  Let's say that you have not interacted with another person for a while and that person meanwhile has changed certain behaviors which had been very irritating to you.  In the next meeting with that person, you may not be operating in the present with that individual, but may have your interaction highly influenced by negatively tinged memories.  The trouble is, with such behavior, we are likely to bring out the insecurities in the other person which brings his or her spirit down and activates the same behavior which we had been annoyed by and on which they had worked to overcome.

Let's take another situation where two people are in an ongoing relationship but are having continued friction.  The fact that the interactions are of low quality is a sign that neither of the two parties is sampling either one's own or the other's freshest and most quality experiences.  In other words, both of them can be seen as walking around mostly on floors away from the upper floors of the library, periodically bumping into each other and sharing unquality, non-fresh information about themselves, each other, or about the world in general.  Thank goodness, such an existence feels bad.

When we are in a peaceful mood is when we want to stack as many volumes in our library as possible.  For example, when in a quality, peaceful mood, we can allow as many sensory inputs as possible by going on a walk like a child would, through seeing, touching, smelling and having everything be experienced through our senses opened and our mind opened to really be able to add many volumes to our upper floors.  Thereby, we move the center of gravity of the memory library up a few floors toward more consistent living in touch with our health.

The more we have sampled the upper floors in terms of the feeling tone and the quality of experience, the more we are able to sense just how unpleasant the lower floors are. While on those lower floors, we become accustomed or familiar to that quality of data and tone to the point, where we may experience it as not especially bothersome. As we become more aware and sensitive, we are better able to discern even small deviations away from our health and listen more knowingly to the vibrations which tip us off to the fact that without knowing, our elevator had been going down.

I am deeply impressed with the fact that when people have gone through highly traumatic experiences, such as the loss of a loved one, divorce, abuse, and even more devastating experiences such as prisoner of war camps, when healing has taken place, they are able to talk about and recall those experiences without becoming emotionally upset. It seems as if they are seeing those experiences now from a higher plane and in a different light, such that they can put such human events in context of their whole life, as opposed to having the traumatic experience be taking center stage in their thoughts and emotions. Does that possibly mean, when someone is recalling a traumatic event with significant pain and anguish, that the pain is more a reflection of their current mood level than of the traumatic event itself? I believe that is the case.

---

A bad memory is not forgetting,
but remembering
the wrong things.

Author unknown

---

"I will remember the works of the Lord, surely I will
remember thy wonders of old.

I will meditate also of all thy work, and talk
of thy doings."

Psalms 77:11,12

When such pain from a memory occurs, we are for some reason vulnerable to again take the event personally or having it overly attached to our current being. It also may reflect that something is left unresolved that needs to truly be forsaken or forgiven. The common element in this whole situation seems to again be the spirit attempting to signal us to be away from the painful past experience, whether by not dwelling on it, due to it not being helpful for our current situation, or through repenting, seeking forgiveness, or forgiving another, so as to not have it encumber us anymore. Stating it in another way, inner pain can be a harmful trap to induce us to blow a memory of the past out of proportion and attach it to our current situation, or it can be a helpful signal to get away from that painful memory or style of thinking, to maximize our ability to live more joyfully and effectively in the present.

Certain memories can be a wonderful source of comfort, warmth, and inspiration. Such memories are found on the upper floors where a pleasant tone is present. In other words, in the mood-related memory library, it is enjoyable to browse, but only on the upper floors. Keep in mind, the upper floors are closer to the Son.

It's okay to browse,
but only
on the
upper floors.

---

Some people
dwell
on the
wrong level.

Ryan Hulbert

# Chapter 5

## Opening Your Heart Through Using Your Senses

Principle #7   WE FUNCTION BETTER WHEN WE TAKE
ADVANTAGE OF A REGULAR FLOW OF NEW INFORMATION
THROUGH OUR SENSES RATHER THAN REPROCESSING OLD
INFORMATION IN OUR THINKING.

> *"This is the Lord's doing; it is marvelous in our eyes.*
> *This is the day which the Lord hath made; we will rejoice and be glad in*
> *it."*
> Psalms 118:23,24

As adults in the modern western world, we think way too much and use our senses way too little.  In contrast, little children are like sensing devices, always relishing opportunities to use each of their five senses of touch, taste, sight, hearing, and smell.  Children, for example, cannot pass by the opportunity on a rainy day to splash in a puddle, delighting in watching the spray, hearing the squeal of others running from the spray, or simply enjoying the feel of the water gush out from under their feet.

Earlier in the book, we discussed how each of our five senses connect first in our brain to the mood centers in the core of the brain and then radiate out toward the cortex, where the information is stored. Perhaps only through a regular flow of fresh input from our senses can our mood center (the heart) remain open and warm.  Let's imagine watching the brain activity of an individual who spends much time thinking, analyzing, and solving problems in his head, to the neglect of regularly engaging in simple and frequent opportunities to sense and enjoy the present, such as "stopping to smell the roses."  While such a person's cortex would have mental activity, his mood center and especially the portion involved with pleasure, would become atrophied and dull from lack of use.

Carl Jung was a famous psychiatrist who was, for a time, a student of Sigmund Freud.  Jung and Freud eventually parted ways, however, due to Freud's view and approach largely focusing on the unhealthy aspects of humans, while Jung emphasized the healthy functioning of the psyche as a primary concern.  He felt that only the healthy psyche could be used as a satisfactory basis from which to understand pathology or unhealthy functioning.  Further, he believed that to be more fully spiritually alive, that much could be gained from the wisdom of other cultures, than that of western Europe.

Come to your senses

---

Open your heart
and
God will open
your eyes.

He was deeply impressed, for example, by a Pueblo chief whom he met on his visit to New Mexico during the winter of 1924-25. The chief described the alarm that white Americans inspired in him: "See how cruel the whites look," he said. "Their lips are thin, their noses sharp, their faces furrowed and distorted by folds. Their eyes have a staring expression; they are always seeking something. What are they seeking? The whites want something, they are always uneasy and restless. We do not know what they want. We do not understand them. We think they are mad." Jung asked him why he thought the whites were mad. "They say they think with their heads," the chief replied. "Why, of course, what do you think with?" Jung asked him in surprise. "We think here," the chief said, indicating his heart.

Jung saw that the emphasis on "head-thinking" had enabled the Europeans to master the world through science, technology and armed might, but that, in the process they had lost the capacity to think with the heart and live through the soul (p. 272, *On Jung*, by Anthony Stevens). Because we as adults tend to think too much, we literally do tone down the ability to perceive with our heart and thereby fuel our souls with inspiration.

This concept was dramatically illustrated in a story I heard from Joel Slack, a young man recovering from schizophrenia, who put on a workshop at the Cherokee Mental Health Institute in 1993. He told the fascinating personal story of him going through a psychotic break while playing basketball in college, and then being in and out of mental hospitals over a several year period while he was actively psychotic. He described many situations in mental hospitals from a patient's point of view, and especially emphasized how confused he was by almost constantly trying to figure out what was wrong and how to cope with the inner tension, the fast moving and unusual thoughts, and feelings of being less than adequate as a person.

i thank You God for most this amazing day;
for the leaping greenly spirits
of trees and a blue true dream of sky; and for
everything which is natural
which is infinite which is yes

(i who have died am alive again today,
and this is the sun's birthday; this is the birth
day of life and of love and wings: and of the gay
great happening illimitable earth)

how should tasting touching hearing seeing
breathing any--lifted from the no
of all nothing--human merely being
doubt unimaginable You?

(now the ears of my ears awake and
now the eyes of my eyes are opened)

e.e. cummings

Most intriguing was Joel's description of certain events which led up to him having breakthroughs in his psychosis, which led to eventual recovery from the psychosis. Once for several days, he was in a catatonic stupor, where he was completely motionless as he concentrated with all his might. Often in such states, people believe that unless they keep a profound concentration going on a particular topic, something very terrible might happen to others or to the world in general. Joel stated that this was his mindset during the time when a nurse came up to his bed and for several minutes, simple placed her open palm on his clothing on his back. At first, her therapeutic touch was experienced by him as an intrusion to his need to concentrate. As she maintained the touch, however, he realized for the first time, in what might have been months, that he was aware of something outside of himself, rather than focusing on his thoughts.

He believes that tapping into this senses was the stimulus for the experience he had shortly thereafter. After getting out of the catatonic state, he was in the hallway of the ward in the mental hospital, and found himself gazing at an old dingy gray hall fan. As he focused on the fan, which allowed him to quiet the normally very busy state of his mind, he was amazed as the dingy gray color began to very slowly take on a light blue tinge. The more he looked at the fan, the more the blue color became brighter and brighter until suddenly he realized he was looking at a bright blue K-Mart fan. He also realized that this perception was actually how the fan looked and that his previous view of it as a dingy gray fan was a distortion of reality.

Joel began to experiment with the phenomenon of quietly visually focusing on items, such as the woven fabric on a chair, attempting to look at the details, such as tiny fibers and patterns. In retrospect, he realized that he was using his senses in such a way as to be incompatible with the very busy thinking which had been going on in his head. More and more as he practiced this new skill, he was able to pull himself away from the misguided use of his thoughts, which had only prolonged his confusion and psychosis.

While I was writing this portion of the book, I shared some of these thoughts with two secretaries at the mental health clinic where I work. Both of them had grown up on a farm and were now living in town. They reflected how living in the country had naturally engaged their senses in many ways, including the barnyard smells, the feel of the dirt, and watching the various cloud formations which were especially interesting during storms. They also talked of their love of camping in the mountains, where they felt so peaceful and where their senses were used so frequently.

We laughed about the fact that it is hard to "think" while in the barnyard. One of them chuckled and said, "That's right, you've got to watch where you are stepping!" Maybe, in fact, we <u>are</u> more fully alive when we are using our senses and taking life one step at a time.

In addition to our five physical senses, we have a nonphysical sixth sense, often referred to as our intuition. Our sixth sense is unique in that it does not bring information in from the outside; its information is from the inside. Various words used to describe the sixth sense reflect the fact that this sense comes from within: <u>in</u>sight, <u>in</u>tuition, <u>in</u>spiration.

By using our five senses more, our heart becomes more open. As our heart is more open, the promptings from within can then easily come to our awareness.

Truth is within ourselves; it takes no rise
From outward things, whate'er you may believe.
There is an inmost centre in us all,
Where truth abides in fullness; and around,
Wall upon wall, the gross flesh hems it in,
This perfect, clear perception--which is truth.

A baffling and perverting carnal mesh
Binds it, and makes all error; and to know,
Rather consists in opening out a way
Whence the imprisoned splendor may escape,
Than in effecting entry for a light
Supposed to be without.

Robert Browning, "Paracelsus" Part 1

# SECTION III

## Loving God with all our Mind.

One of the difficulties of more fully experiencing our true worth in this life is due to the fact that the true nature of each of us is immortal and we are currently in a mortal existence. Mortal is synonymous with temporal, which in turn, is synonymous with time. In other words, we are eternal beings currently in a time-oriented world. Through our conscious mind, we interact with aspects of our existence, which are not time-oriented. The next section of the book is an attempt to help us more fully love God with all of our mind, both conscious and unconscious. The following chapter will focus on how we can be in time, without being of time, in order to more fully experience our true worth.

# Chapter 6

## In Time But Not of Time

Principle #8  WE CAN BEST BE ENLIGHTENED WHEN IN THE PRESENT MOMENT

*"For thou wilt light my candle.  The Lord my God will enlighten my darkness.*
Psalms 18:28

While conducting my doctoral dissertation, during the research fellowship in Belgium, I was impressed to learn how closely associated our self concept is with time.  Our self concept is not who we really are, but who we think we are.  It was interesting to know that developmental psychologists view our self concept as "gelling" around age seven or eight. Prior to that age, I like to think of children's self concept as similar to a gelatin dessert which has not quite fully set up.  Prior to gelatin setting up, many things can be added, such as shredded carrots or sliced fruits.  After the gelatin has set up, fruit or other items simply bounce off or require more effort to have them stick.  This is not to say that self concept cannot be changed after age seven or eight, but simply that it is more difficult and less malleable.

Corresponding with this gelling of the self concept, is the child's beginning understanding of the nature of time.  It is as if an eternal spirit takes a while to get used to living in a time-oriented world.  As adults, we also use time in the construction of our self concept.  As adults, we view our self concept largely in terms of what we have accomplished in the past, what we wish we had but did not, and in terms of what we did do and wish we had not.  Based on this view of ourselves constructed from our past experiences, we project that image into the future which further contributes to who we think we are, based on imagining what we are and are not capable of doing in the future.

Thank goodness our self concept never does quite fit, because it is a more or less distorted view of who we really are.  Even if someone has had a "charmed life," with all the accomplishments, possessions, and acclaim anyone would ever want, there is still a sense of discomfort related to the questions such as, "How long will this last?" What will people think of me if I cannot keep this up?"  The world has developed such distorted high standards in beauty, income, and accomplishments, that if we adopt such standards, essentially nobody can feel good about themselves.

While studying time and self concept on the research fellowship, I attempted to, in picture form, show how time, self concept, and eternity are related. The best that I would come up with was that eternity was similar to the vanishing point at the end of a straight highway. In other words, I attempted to equate eternity with the concept of infinity or the boundless "end point" of a line in either direction. Such an explanation was never very satisfying to me, mostly because I know that God exists in eternity, and if eternity existed in some far off future or past location, how could that explain the experience such as feeling God's presence <u>now</u> or receiving answers from God in prayer <u>now</u>.

A major breakthrough in my attempts to situate time, self concept and eternity occurred when a good friend of mind in Iowa, Jim White, commented on some writing I had done concerning this dilemma. He said it appears that the present is where eternity is, referred me to the interesting book by C.S. Lewis, *The Screwtape Letters*, and shortly thereafter gave me a copy of that book as a birthday present.

What Jim White was referring to is found in the beginning of chapter 15 of *The Screwtape Letters*. This book was written during World War II and is a fictional account of a senior devil, Screwtape, who is writing to his nephew, Wormwood, who had his first assignment to bedevil a mortal "patient." The first portion of that chapter is quoted below.

My Dear Wormwood,

I had noticed, of course, that the humans were having a lull in their European war--what they naively call "The War"!--and am not surprised that there is a corresponding lull in the patient's anxieties. Do we want to encourage this, or to keep him worried? Tortured fear and stupid confidence are both desirable states of mind. Our choices between them raise important questions.

The humans live in time but our Enemy destines them to eternity. He, therefore, I believe, wants them to attend chiefly to two things, to eternity itself, and to that point of time which they call the Present.

**For the Present is the point at which time touches eternity...**

Our business is to get them away from the eternal and from the Present.

(The Screwtape Letters, p. 76-77, emphasis added)

I believe that it is true that in our temporal, time-oriented existence, the only place where we can experience a connection to eternity is in the present moment (see Diagram 14).

It is, as if, the only place our eternal spirit has breathing room and can be fully functional, is in the realm where eternity intersects with our temporal experience. I like to think of the present moment as the only dot on the time line of life that is different from all the others. It may often look just like the other dots, but when examined closely, it is the only one that has as if a tiny pinprick of the light of life coming through it. When used properly, the present moment is like the pupil of the eye or the iris (shutter) of a camera which can open up to let more light come through. This light is not a physical thing received as if light coming into our eyes, but it is like a spiritual light coming from eternity passing through us and being projected out to illuminate our vision. (see Diagram 15).

As can be seen in the diagram, when the present moment is open, the rays from eternity where the sun is always shining, can come through. It is beautiful to realize that when our conduit to eternity is open, our true self worth is what we feel and experience and not the limited time related self concept.

# Diagram 14

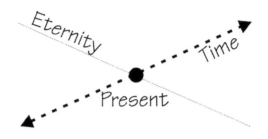

Christ stands at the door
and knocks.
He is in eternity
and
our door to eternity
we must open to receive him
while in mortality
is in the present.

Ryan Hulbert

# Diagram 15

The influence of Eternity, connects with us
in the present moment, but can only come
into us if our minds are open and clear.

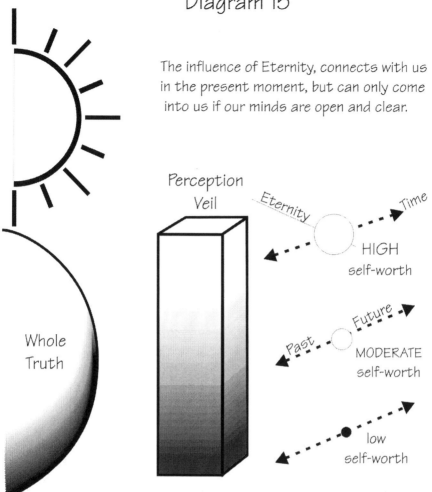

"Commit thy way unto the Lord; trust also in him; and he shall bring
forth thy righteousness as the light, and thy judgement as the noonday."
Psalms 37:56

I believe that our true worth is totally unrelated to our accomplishments, whether past or future, but is based rather on God's unconditional love for each of us. When we see through the "eye of faith," we understand this more clearly than when we see "through a glass darkly" and we begin to know, even as also we are known. (1Corinthians13:12).

Let's further examine what I am attempting to describe as the "present." I am using this term to describe the exact instant or moment in which we are now living. This is in contrast to the use of the term "present" for our current situation, the current day, or even the current hour or minute. These terms describe a time frame which is much too broad to describe the experience of being totally present in the moment. I would like to contend that the current moment is the only place where, for us as individuals, "real life" is happening in its fullest sense. I like to think of opening a present moment as similar to placing a warm fingertip on a frost-covered window to melt a small peephole, to then be able to see outside more clearly.

Abraham Maslow, a famous psychologist, coined the term "peak experience" to describe beautiful, soul expanding experiences, which have a timeless element and greatly increase one's inner security and wholeness as a person and loving connectedness to others. Making a play on words, I like to think of learning to open up the present moment as a "peek experience," where we are able to open the window of the present, which is the only place where our eternal worth can be more fully appreciated.

Let me attempt to distinguish between living in the moment, as opposed to what can be described as living for the moment. Living in the moment, means having an eye on eternity and being open to the guidance of the Spirit, to most effectively handle that which we are currently experiencing. Living in such a fashion, involves placing our trust in the Lord and being willing to follow his commandments, even when it may not logically make sense to do so. In contrast, living for the moment involves an impulsive seeking of gratification with no regard to the eternal laws of God (see Diagram 16).

# Diagram 16

What we Experience

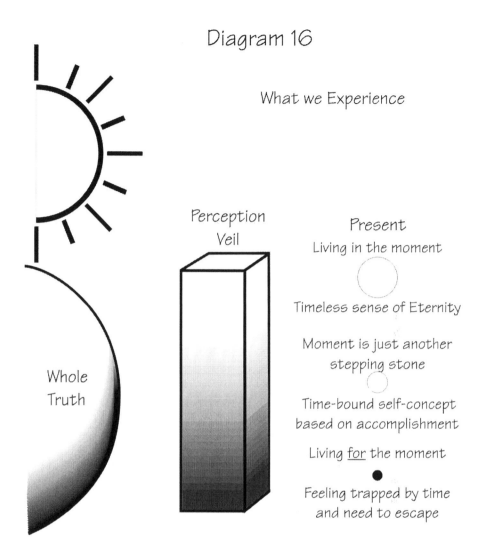

Perception
Veil

Present
Living in the moment

Timeless sense of Eternity

Moment is just another
stepping stone

Time-bound self-concept
based on accomplishment

Living _for_ the moment

Feeling trapped by time
and need to escape

Whole
Truth

"Be still, and know that I am God: I will be exalted among the heathen, I will be exalted in the earth."

Psalms 46:10

There is an enjoyable little book entitled *The Precious Present* by Spencer Johnson, M.D., which in short story form emphasizes the freeing nature of living in the present. In that book, Dr. Johnson states: "It is wise for me to think about the past and to learn from my past, but it is not wise for me to be in the past. For that is how I lose myself. It is also wise to think about my future and to prepare for my future, but it is not wise for me to be in the future. For that, too, is how I lose myself." (The Precious Present, p. 48 & 49).

A similar thought is echoed by Ralph Waldo Emerson: "Finish every day and be done with it. You have done what you could: some blunders and absurdities crept in: forget them as soon as you can. Tomorrow is a new day; you shall begin it serenely and with too high a spirit to be encumbered with your old nonsense." Bill Wilson, one of the founders of Alcoholics Anonymous, commented on the notion of the AA theme of living "one day at a time:" The idea of 'twenty-four hour' living applies primarily to the emotional life of the individual. Emotionally speaking, we must not live in yesterday or in tomorrow" (The AA Way of Life, 1967, p. 287). Although I would contend that living in the current day is too broad of a time unit for most effective emotional well being, it is still much more effective than attempting to live in tomorrow or yesterday.

# Chapter 7

## Feelings and Emotions

Principle #9 PLEASANT FEELINGS TELL US THAT WE ARE IN THE MOMENT AND IRRITATING EMOTIONS TELL US THAT WE ARE OUT OF THE MOMENT

.

> *"For God hath not given us the spirit of fear;*
> *but of power, and of love, and of a sound mind."*
> 2 Timothy 1:7

For every day language we usually use the words "feelings" and "emotions" interchangeably; just like we use the words "insects" and "bugs" interchangeably. Among the few things I have taught my wife, compared to the many things that she has taught me in our marriage, has been an appreciation for bugs. I must say that she has not gained the full appreciation for them that I would like her to, but she has made progress over the years.

As a child and youth, I very much enjoyed studying creepy-crawly things in general and among other things enjoyed watching insects, including earning the insect study merit badge in Boy Scouts. Technically speaking, the term bug is reserved for a crawling insect with a pointed beak for piercing and sucking. Bugs either have no wings or have a front pair of wings thickened at the base. We often use the term bug to describe any insect or other animal somewhat similar such as ants, spiders, beetles, and centipedes. By pointing out to my wife some of the differences in these various creatures, she was better able to appreciate the difference between "good" bugs and "bad" bugs. To her, the distinction largely continues to be the location of the creature: That is, whether they are in or out of the house.

In actuality, there are no good bugs and bad bugs, but only bugs with different purposes. It is true that some are , in general, more bothersome than others, but, still have their particular purpose. Such is also the case with feelings. There really are not bad or good feelings, but some are pleasant and others are bothersome. At this point, I would like to draw what I believe is a very important distinction between types of feelings, to the point of giving them different labels. I would like to reserve the term "feelings" for that which we experience when we are allowing our mind to live in the present. When we are focused on the present and our mind is relaxed, we experience feelings such as happiness,

Joy
is the flag
of the castle of the heart
which is flown
when the
King
is in residence.
C.S. Lewis

hope, joy, peace, serenity, warmth, love and enthusiasm.  I have recently learned, for example, that the word enthusiasm comes from the Greek root word "entheos."  The "theos" portion of the word means "God" and the "en" portion of the word means "in".  Thus, when we feel enthusiasm, the influence of God is in us.  In contrast, when our present is pinched off and our connection with eternity has been closed, we "lose" our enthusiasm because the realm in which such feelings are felt has been constricted.

In contrast to feelings, I want to propose the use of the word "emotions" for that which we experience when our minds have been allowed to be diverted from the present moment where our spirit cannot be fully alive, and thus our spirit lets us know that it does not like the reduction of its freedom and the possibility of its guidance (see Diagram 17).

Notice that the word "emotions" has the word "motion" in it.  I like to describe emotions as "motion-indicators" signaling that we have strayed from the sure path where our best self can be fully functional.

Perhaps you have driven on a highway where outside of the white lines, along the side of the highway were ridges purposely built into the asphalt along the outer edge of the road.  These ridges, which I will refer to as "rumble strips" were constructed to be irritating for a purpose.  That purpose, of course, is to alert us when we are going off of the road when we are distracted or falling asleep, that we are potentially getting into trouble and could be about to crash if we are not careful.  Bothersome emotions are like these rumble strips to warn us when we have strayed away from the present which is where the spirit can have the most smooth sailing.  It is, as if, the spirit becomes rubbed the wrong way when we are using our mind in ways which are unhelpful in dealing with our situations and unproductive in handling our challenges.

Picture, if you will, a band of rumble strips several feet wide along both sides of a highway.  Outside of that relatively narrow band of rumble strips, picture progressively larger sets of bumps until they are the size of speed bumps. These bumps would be there to jar us in case the smaller rumble strips had not fully gotten our attention.  These larger bumps are comparable to more intense, bothersome emotions which are attempting to warn us even more vigorously that not only have we strayed from helpful thoughts, but we have strayed way too far.

According to this comparison, not only do both sides of the highway have these increasingly jarring rumble strips, there is even a different type of signal to tell us off of which side of the road we have strayed.  For example, let's say we were driving in total darkness, feeling our way only through the smoothness of the highway or the vibrations from the rumble strips.  Due to the different types of vibrations, we could determine whether we were off to the left or off to the right. Let's compare veering off the left, to attempting to live in the past, veering off the right to attempting to live in the future, and being on the highway to fully showing up for life in the present (see Diagram 18).

A famous psychologist, Fritz Perls, once said, "Unfortunately, most people rarely show up for their life while it is being lived." When I first heard that statement, I personally could really relate to it, because I realized that I had spent many years not fully showing up for life. All of us are out of alignment, at least somewhat, and I tend to be out of alignment to the right. In other words, out of good intentions and through not knowing any better, I have often let my mind drift toward attempting to live in the future, thereby reducing my ability to more appreciate and take advantage of present living. Before more carefully examining the motion indicators concerning the future, let's examine the emotions or motion indicators that are given to warn us that we have veered to the left or have attempted to live in the past.

# Diagram 17

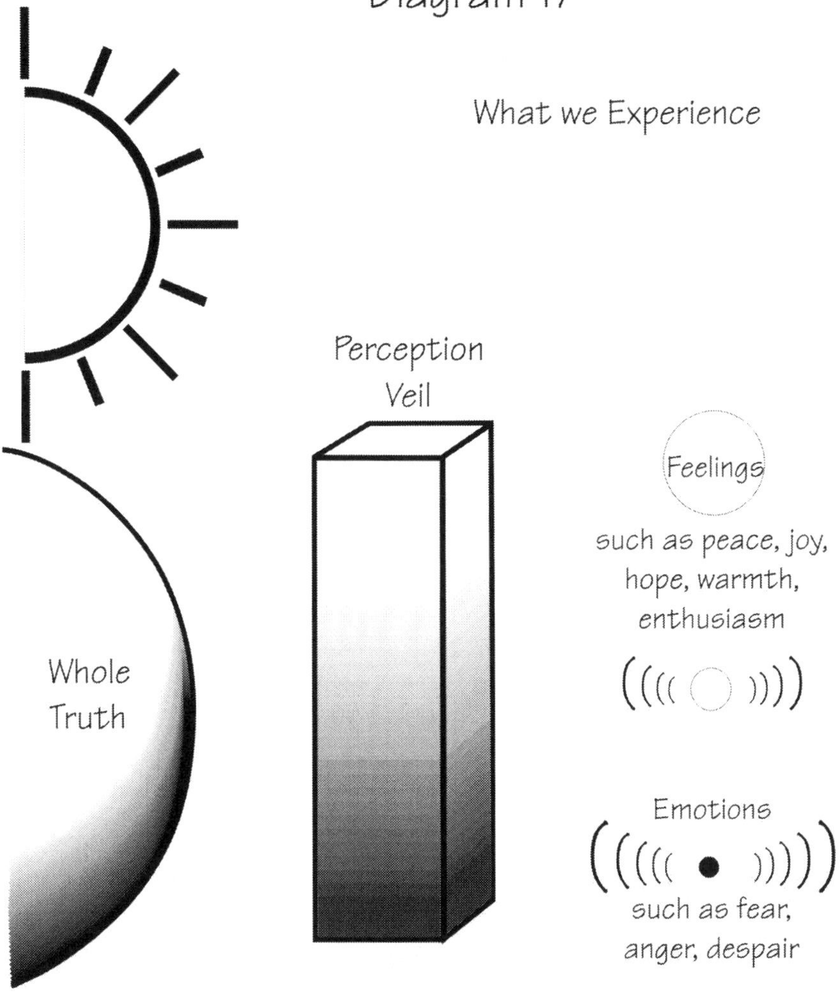

What we Experience

Perception
Veil

Feelings

such as peace, joy,
hope, warmth,
enthusiasm

$((((\bigcirc))))$

Whole
Truth

Emotions

$(((((\bullet)))))$

such as fear,
anger, despair

"Acquaint now thyself with him (the Lord), and be at peace: thereby good shall come unto thee."

Job 22:21

"Thou wilt keep him in perfect peace whose mind is stayed on thee: because he trusteth in thee."

Isaiah 26:3

A negative emotion
is immediate feedback
that we are thinking
in a way that is interfering
with our happiness
and taking away our
self-esteem.
author unknown

# Diagram 18

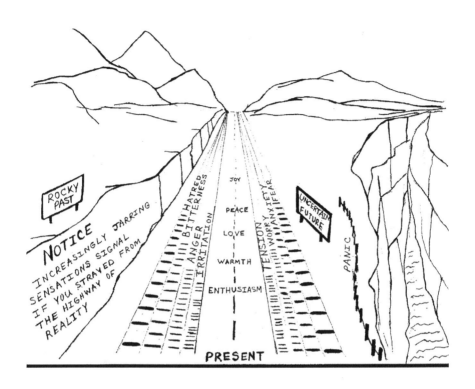

"Now the end of the commandment is charity out of a pure heart, and of a good conscience, and of faith unfeigned. From which some having <u>swerved</u> have turned aside unto vain jangling."

1 Timothy 1:5,6;
emphasis added

## Attempting to live in the Past

Guilt is a past-oriented rumble strip to signal us that we have behaved in ways that move us away from the warmth of God through reducing our access to the Light of Christ. The irritation from guilt is to induce us to discontinue engaging in such behavior. Misinterpreting the unpleasant sensations from guilt can result in a person believing they are of less worth, and thereby leave the person more vulnerable to either repeating or doing other forms of unhealthy and sinful behavior. It is interesting that a Hebrew word for sin is "hata," which means "to miss the mark."

It is very important, at this point, to emphasize how Satan, the father of darkness, can confuse us when we are riding on the rumble strips. The mere fact that we are having a vigorously jarring experience when we are riding on the rumble strips, can trick us, through its intensity, to perceive what we are thinking at the time is highly important. In other words, the more intense the emotions, the more the unhealthy thoughts tend to be blown out of proportion. The mental trap is that the jarring sensation, which is actually an attempt by our spirit to let us know that we are off-base, can, when we are not aware of that fact, result in us putting even more emphasis on the off-base thinking.

Anger is another past-oriented rumble strip. It is not possible to have the "last straw" unless all of the other straws have been held in mind and, at least periodically focused on. The smaller rumble strips on the anger dimension are mild irritation, with increasing intensity to anger, then bitterness, which can really jar our bolts loose, and finally to the ultimate distorted emotion of hatred. When we hear of a "blow up" between people, it is the result of people being unaware of the purpose of the intensity of the signal as a warning, and thereby being caught up in the trap of blowing the irritation out of proportion. (see Diagram 19.)

86

# Diagram 19

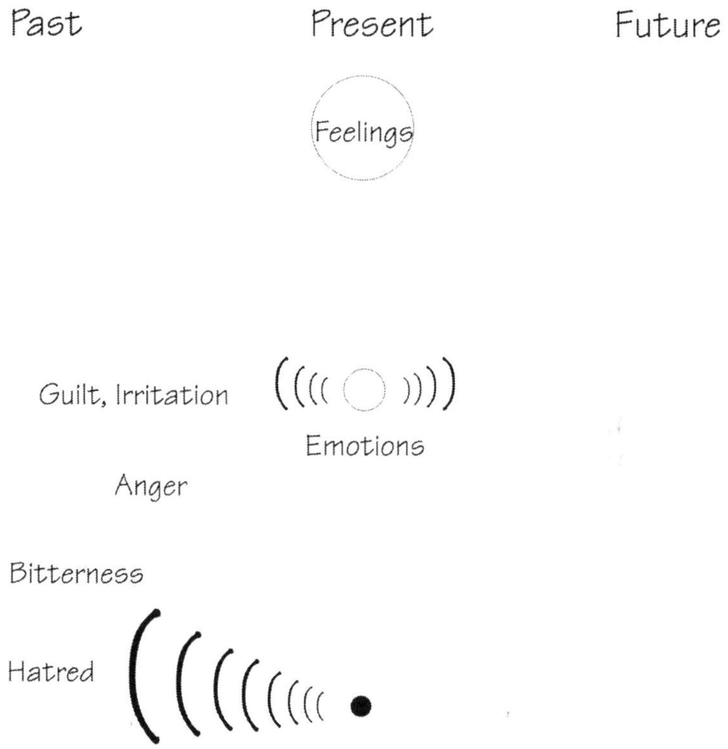

Past
Present
Future
Feelings
Guilt, Irritation
Emotions
Anger
Bitterness
Hatred


"He that is slow to wrath is of great understanding: but he that is hasty of spirit exalteth folly."

Proverbs 14:2

"He that is soon angry dealeth foolishly."

Proverbs 14:17

Everyone has been hurt.
It's what you do with it
that makes a difference.
                    Sidney Simon

---

It's okay to look back--
    just don't stare.
                    Sidney Simon

## Attempting to live in the Future

I have had my share of riding on the past oriented rumble strips, but I am especially familiar with the right-hand or future-oriented rumble strips. These also grow in intensity through increasingly jarring signals the further away the person is straying from the road. The first is a sense of tension when we have attempted to live, at least somewhat, ahead of where real life is happening. The signal grows in intensity to the bothersome signal of worry. I am very familiar with worry and have spent many years of my life with one set of tires on the worry rumble strips. I did not know any better, but for some reason felt my life was meant to be always, at least somewhat, full of tension or worry, or it was as if, I was not doing my full share if I wasn't tense or worried. Whenever something might lull me over into the present, such as a hobby, sport, or some other engaging activity, it wasn't too long before a thought that was not worth thinking came along such as, "You're being lazy." Out of what I thought was my duty, I would then say to myself, "Okay, it was nice while it lasted," and then go back to living in the future in my thoughts. I would then be bumping along the side of the road, mentally patting myself on the back with thoughts such as, "This isn't easy, but, at least I'm not being lazy!"

Beyond the worry rumble strips, the more jarring emotions of anxiety, and then fear are experienced. About here on the anxiety rumble strips, is where the body attempts to warn us where we are by the heart thumping noticeably (see Diagram 20). Without knowing what this signal is all about, we again can become trapped, that what we are thinking about must be of tremendous importance to be accompanied by our heart even physically reacting. In such conditions, if we let our mind run away with us, that which we are anxiously thinking about becomes embellished and more vivid. This, in turn, results in more and more jarring emotions, which are actually attempting to warn us to return to the only place where we can do anything about our concerns--the Present.

On the furthest most edge of the future-oriented rumble strips is an intense warning, which we call a panic attack. This is when our heart beats so fast that people describe it like a heart attack or as if their heart is going to beat out of their chest. Another common panic symptom is the extremely frightening sensation of not being able to get enough breath, which results in a panic reaction of hyperventilating and, at times, passing out. I would like to compare panic attacks to a guard rail along the side of the highway which we smack up against when we have gone way too far off the road. People often seek mental health services after experiencing a panic attack. They will state something along the lines of, "I was really scared by this experience and really need to manage my life differently." I like to translate what they are saying to, "I have been living in the future way too long and way too far off of the road."

When I was attempting to use these notions to help a patient in Iowa, who was suffering from much anxiety, he said, "Do you want to know how wide my road is?" He gestured holding his thumb and index finger about two inches wide and continued, "My road is about this big, just barely big enough for my bicycle tires. Even with that, I can't hardly keep on it and spend almost all of my day swerving back and forth on the rumble strips from sadness to fear. Then there are times when it's like my road has totally pinched off and then I'm riding my bicycle, but now it's like I'm between the railroad tracks riding my bicycle on the ties." I thought what a graphic way of describing the almost constant jarring that this man has experienced as he was attempting to hold on for dear life.

In times of insecurity, our road literally can begin to narrow in front of our eyes, to the point of the rumble strips becoming closer together, to the point of having our wheels on both sides riding on the rumble strips, with us straddling the relatively narrow road. At times like those, we need to first of all, take our foot off the accelerator, slow down, keep following the narrow road and not make any sudden moves. Through not letting our mind run away with us, with practice, we can return our thoughts to the present with an accompanying widening of the road before our very eyes, while the motion indicator rumble strips continue to flank the road, but while we travel the smooth road with the accompanying enriching feelings.

In conclusion of this section in discussing the difference between emotions and feelings, I would like to remind us of the common childhood game which I know simply as the "Warmer-Warmer-Cooler-Cooler Game." You are probably familiar with this game, where a small object is hidden in a room and another person is directed to the object simply by stating whether or not the direction the person is moving is either getting warmer-warmer or cooler-cooler. Only by having the person who is looking for the object continue to move and make attempts to find the object, can the person giving the directions continue to say whether they are on-track or off-track. It is a fun game and it is amazing how quickly most people can be helped in finding the object, if the person looking continues to move and the person giving the directions gives very frequent signals.

When I use this game as an object lesson in therapy, I ask people how the signals of cooler-cooler helped them to find the object. They invariably say something like, "It told me I was going in the wrong direction." When asked how the warmer-warmer signal helped them, they say, "It helped me know that I was going in the right direction." Thus it is with emotions and feelings. Both are necessary to help us find that which we are looking for. I think that the warmer-warmer-cooler-cooler game is God's favorite game. He plays it with us as His children all the time. The emotions are the cooler-cooler. The feelings are the warmer-warmer.

Lilly's Loose

Lilly is the operator at the switchboard of my brain.
And when she starts reacting, my life becomes insane.
She's supposed to be employed by me--and play a passive role,
But anytime I'm insecure---Lilly takes control.

Lilly's loose, Lilly's loose, Lilly's loose today.
Tell everyone around me just to clear out of my way.
The things I say won't make much sense--all COMMON SENSE is lost.
'Cause when Lilly's at the switchboard--my wires all get crossed.

Lilly is my own creation, thought I needed her with me
To organize and then recall all my life's history.
But she started taking liberty with all my information.
And whenever she starts plugging in--I get a bad sensation.

Lilly's loose, Lilly's loose, Lilly's loose today.
Tell all my friends and relatives to clear out of my way.
I don't give hugs and kisses when I'm in this frame of mind.
And please don't take me seriously--it'd be a waste of time.

She looks out through my eyeballs and sees what I do see,
Then hooks up wires to my past--she thinks she's helping me!
When I'm in a good mood, I can smile at her endeavor.
But when I'm in a bad mood--Lilly's boss, and is she clever.
I'm feeling very scattered--I'm lost in my emotion.
Lilly's on a rampage, and she's causing a commotion.

Sue Pettit

# Diagram 20

"The Lord is my light and my salvation; whom shall I fear? The Lord is the strength of my life; of whom shall I be afraid."

Psalms 27:1

"There is no fear in love; but perfect love casteth out fear: because fear hath torment."

1 John 4:18

"Boast not thyself of tomorrow; for thou knowest not what a day may bring forth."

Proverbs 27:1

| | |
|---|---|
| **F** | **False** |
| **E** | **Evidence** |
| **A** | **Appearing** |
| **R** | **Real** |
| | author unknown |

Fear knocked at the door--

Faith answered it,

And no one was there.

author unknown

# THUNDERDROPS OR RAINDROPS

We were driving down a country road, my son Daniel and I.
As we drove the day got darker, gray clouds rolled across the sky.
Soon any sight of winter sun was lost out of our view.
As the last ray disappeared, young Danny's smile did too.

Great rain drops started splashing and they seemed to cause alarm
To the little boy beside me. He sat close and hugged my arm.
I looked down upon the little head he buried in my side.
I could feel him start to tremble and his eyes were open wide.

Are those THUNDERDROPS?" he asked me. I had never heard
that word.
Thunderdrops, he said, were raindrops seen before the thunder's
heard.
Thunder was a scary thing to him. Its noise filled him with dread.
And when he saw the raindrops fall, scary thoughts raced in his head.

The more he thought his scary thoughts, the more he felt his fears.
We did not hear it thunder, yet his eyes filled up with tears.
He didn't need the thunder now to rumble in the skies.
It was real to him already as his thoughts became his eyes.

We all have our own thunderdrops--a word, a sound, a phrase.
And when they come into our life, we get lost in our own maze.
Like Dan, we see beyond our eyes and live in thought's illusions.
The emotions caught inside these thoughts then color our delusions.

How many times I wonder? How many moments lost?
By things we think might happen--our sanity the cost.
Thunderdrops are only raindrops, wrapped inside a troubled thought.
When you understand the wrapping, you're less likely to get caught.

Sue Pettit

94

God should be our
steering wheel,
not just our
spare tire.

# Chapter 8

## Three Fuels

Principle #10  EVERY THOUGHT WE THINK MAKES A DIFFERENCE IN CONTRIBUTING TO OR DETRACTING FROM OUR WELL-BEING AND SENSE OF CLOSENESS TO GOD.

*"Casting down imaginations, and every high thing that exalteth itself against the knowledge of God and bringing into captivity every thought to the obedience of Christ."*
2 Corinthians 10:5

In February 1993, I was fortunate to attend a three day workshop in Washington State with George Pransky, who is one of the main trainers in the United States concerning "The Three Principles." The principles are Mind, thought, and consciousness. I have come to view "Mind" as God's thoughts, "thought" as our thoughts, and "consciousness" as our awareness of the relative difference between our thoughts and God's thoughts. (Keep in mind Isaiah 55:8,9, describing God's thoughts being higher than our thoughts). In that training, I was especially impressed with an analogy he used to compare whether we are mostly living in the past, present, or future through three different types of fuels. He described that just as certain machines are built for certain types of fuel, we, as humans, were built for a particular very refined fuel which he entitled the <u>Fuel of Inspiration</u>. This is what our being wants to be fueled by and what brings about the smoothest functioning. When using this fuel of inspiration, we feel more fully alive and are open to insights and inspiration to live our life most effectively or to creatively deal with troubled areas. He drew this Fuel of Inspiration as a circle flanked on either side by somewhat smaller circles, which represented cheap alternative fuels which we, as humans, tend to use. We can use them temporarily without undue damage, but prolonged use of these cheap alternative fuels leads to malfunctioning.

The effects of using the cheap alternative fuels are very comparable to the effects of hitting the rumble strips on either side of the highway which warn us when we are off base. One of these cheap alternative fuels, which we use when we are attempting to live in the past, Dr. Pransky entitled <u>Fossil Fuel</u>. The other fuel, which is what we use when we attempt to live in the future, he entitled <u>Fuel of Imagination</u>. When we use the cheap alternative fuels, the Fuel of Inspiration becomes reduced, comparable to the center circle becoming smaller and one or both of the other circles becoming larger (see Diagram 21).

I would like to elaborate on Dr. Pransky's concept of these three fuels. When we experience feelings as described in the previous chapter, we are at that moment being fueled by inspiration. When we are experiencing bothersome emotions, we are fueling our being by one or both of the cheap alternative fuels, depending on which direction our thoughts are more off the mark of the present. These cheaper "man-made" fuels add pollution to the air which, in turn, makes the air heavier, leading to a sinking mood experience. In contrast, the Fuel of Inspiration is not of this world and has anti-gravity characteristics, which causes our mood to rise and our spirit to soar. The relative mixture of these fuels makes a big difference in our ability to rise above our challenges. Just as a balloon full of pure helium rises better than one with a mixture of helium and regular air, the higher percentage of moments we spend each day being fueled by the more pure Fuel of Inspiration, the greater our enjoyment and effectiveness.

The only place we can breathe is in the present. We cannot breathe in the past and we cannot breathe in the future. Similarly, the only place we can be fully alive is living in the present, when our being is fueled by its proper Fuel of Inspiration. It is interesting to know that the word "spirit" comes from the Latin "spirare," which means "to breathe."

On the day that I was writing this portion of the book, my mother gave me a poster that she had bought from a child who was selling things door-to-door, as part of a fund raising project. She knew of my fascination with the idea of living in the present and thus was excited to buy a particular poster with the message below:

**I was regretting the past and fearing the future**
**Suddenly my Lord was speaking:  My name is I Am**
**He paused, I waited.  He continued.**
**When you live in the past with its mistakes and regrets, it is hard.**
**I am not there.**
**My name is not I Was.**
**When you live in the future with its problems and fears, it is hard.**
**I am not there.**
**My name is not I Will Be.**
**When you live in this moment, it is not hard.**
**I am here.**
**My name is I Am.**
Helen Mallicoat

# Diagram 21

Inspired
Clear
thoughts

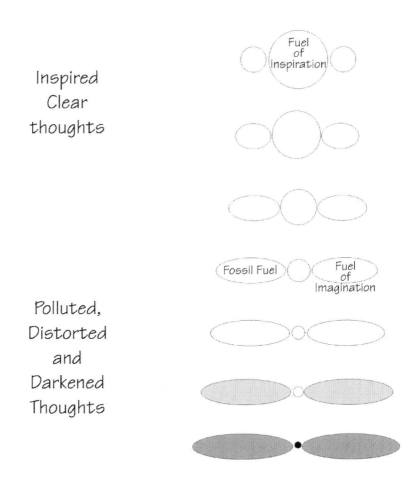

Polluted,
Distorted
and
Darkened
Thoughts

"I will instruct thee and teach thee in the way which thou shall go: I will guide thee with mine eye."

Psalms 32:8

One of the best ways to love God with all of our mind, is to allow our mind to be open to the eternal connection of the present. When we do that, we have a sense of a soaring spirit and are not so weighed down by the pressures of time. When we think of the words "time" and "temporal" being synonymous, I like to also view the word "tempt" as a means of the adversary to "temporalize us," or in other words, lasso us or put a heavy chain on us to drag us down from a more spiritual, timeless sense into a lower, temporal or time oriented experience.

When we drop down to the point where the present is pinched off (see Diagram 22), then we have the experience of the present moment simply being one more dot on the time line of life. Correspondingly the influence of Fossil Fuel and Fuel of Imagination balloon out so that they are the only sources of fuel available to us. Notice how when the present is pinched off and the cheap alternative fuels are in full force, the figure looks like eyeglasses. Truly life looks very different to us when the present is pinched off, as opposed to being open as is shown in the upper part of the diagram. Notice how when the present is pinched off, the focusing on the past and the future becomes joined. In such states of mind, we have the emotions running back and forth from anger to fear, which contributes to a sense of sadness. In such painful experiences, we assume that difficulties from the past will continue in the future, which deflates our hopefulness. Let's compare this situation to being bound not only on a timeline, but in a time pipe similar to a sewer pipe. If we are in a sewer pipe, and we see the flow coming from the past, there is no way to escape, because the flow will continue into the future. There is, however, one slice of pipe and one slice only that is not pipe. What it actually is, is like a valve of the present, which when opened, first of all stops the flow from the past. When the flow of the past is stopped, the future end of the pipe is empty and open for change and not just "more of the same."

As a combination of the cheap alternative fuels is used for a prolonged period of time, the mood of the person progressively drops from sadness to depression. The pressure felt when we are depressed is intense and is an indication of how far we are away from where our spirit wants to be. The deeper the depression, the more intense the agitation and symptoms. These symptoms can include sleep disturbance, backaches, and social withdrawal. All of these unpleasant symptoms are attempting to get our attention to not believe the dark and distorted thoughts, which naturally occur on such low levels. When depression is experienced, although the intensity of the cheap fuels makes our low quality hopeless thoughts seem very believable, there is still present an inner prompting that our perceptions and thoughts just do not make full sense (see Diagram 23).

# Diagram 22

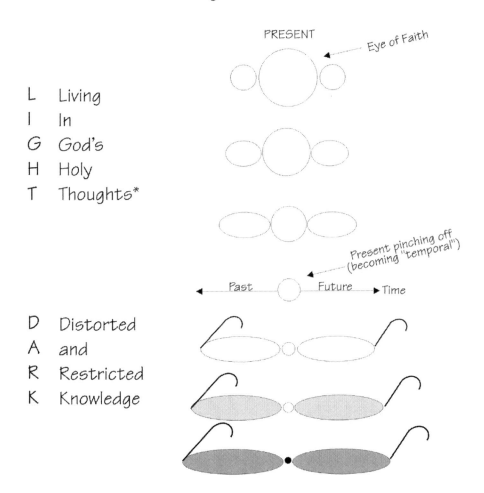

L   Living
I   In
G   God's
H   Holy
T   Thoughts*

D   Distorted
A   and
R   Restricted
K   Knowledge

"For now we see through a glass, darkly; but then face to face: now I know in part; but then shall I know even as also I am known."                                    1 Corinthians 13:12

"Where the Spirit of the Lord is, there is liberty. But we all, with open face beholding as in a glass the glory of the Lord, are changed into the same image from glory to glory, even as by the Spirit of the Lord." 2 Corinthians 3:17, 18

*Found in <u>You Can't Afford a Negative Thought</u>, by John Roger and Peter McWilliams.

**H**    **Help**

**O**    **Open**

**P**    **People's**

**E**    **Eyes**

Quote created by one of my clients, Linda J.

# Diagram 23

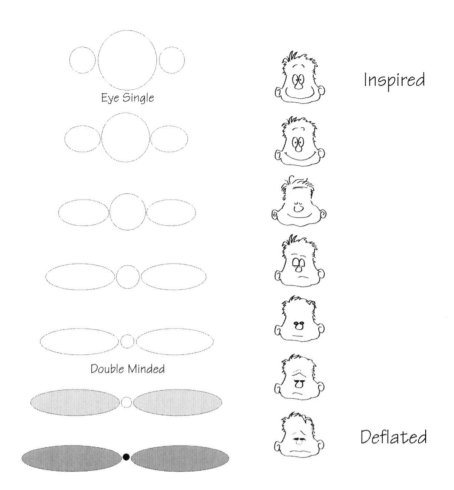

Eye Single

Double Minded

Inspired

Deflated

"The light of the body is the eye: therefore when thine eye is single, thy whole body also is full of light; but when thine eye is evil, thy body also is full of darkness. Take heed therefore that the light which is in thee be not darkness."

St. Luke 11:34, 35

"A double minded man is unstable in all his ways."

James 1:8

The experience described above is clearly stated by Gerald G. Jampolsky in his book, *Out of Darkness into the Light* (p. 67): "When I am depressed, somewhere deep inside, I know that I am denying the presence of God." We miss the mark and sin when we believe untruths, such as we are of little worth or have no hope. In such situations we are similar to the people in the days of Jeremiah, who would "bow for lies: but they are not valiant for the truth upon the earth; for they proceed from evil to evil and they know not me, said the Lord" (Jeremiah 9:3)

Rather than believe the untruths when in a depressed state of mind, among other things we need to "gird up the loins of the mind" (1 Peter 1:13) to fix our faith on guidelines and promises found in the scriptures such as:

"Let thine eyes look right on, and let thine eyelids look straight before thee.
Turn not to the right had nor to the left; remove thy foot from evil."
Proverbs 4:25, 27


"And I will bring the blind by a way that they knew not: I will lead them in paths that
they have not known: I will make darkness light before them, and crooked things straight.
These things will I do unto them, and not forsake them."
Isaiah 42:16

# SECTION IV

## Loving God With All Your Soul

The dictionary defines the word "soul" as the part of the human being that thinks, feels, and makes the body act (World Book Dictionary, 1976). This fourth and final section of the book will focus on practical suggestions for keeping our hearts open, our minds enlightened, and our bodies acting, thereby using our whole being to more fully love God and bless those around us.

When King David appointed his son Solomon to build a temple, he gave Solomon advice, which is applicable to all of us: "Know thou the God of thy father, and serve him with a perfect heart and with a willing mind: for the Lord searcheth all hearts, and understandeth all the imaginations of the thoughts; if thou seek him, he will be found of thee" (1 Chronicles 28:9, emphasis added).

# Chapter 9

## Filling Your Own Lamp

*"Then shall the kingdom of heaven be likened unto ten virgins,
which took their lamps, and went forth to meet the bridegroom. And five
of them were wise, and five were foolish. They that were foolish took their
lamps, and took no oil with them. But the wise took oil in their vessels with
their lamps."*
St. Matthew 25:1-4

Each of us need to individually maintain a supply of spiritual fuel
on hand to be prepared for whatever situation may arise. I am reminded of
this each time I am on a commercial airline and hear the safety instructions,
prior to the flight. Perhaps you have had the same experience that I have
when the flight attendant describes what to do if the cabin in the plane
becomes depressurized and the oxygen masks fall from their
compartments. At that point in the instructions, the guideline is given that
if you are traveling with a small child, first put on your own oxygen mask,
and then assist your child. Each time I hear those instructions, it is food for
thought. I suppose that the guideline is given for two reasons: One, that it
is the correct thing to do, and secondly, it goes against our initial protective
impulses.

In this chapter, a number of suggestions will be given, each of
which are a source of adding drops of proper fuel to our being. This is by
no means a comprehensive list, and the reader is encouraged to experiment
with these ideas and others, which you may already be doing or may later
become aware of. Through the gradual and individualized implementation
of such guidelines as a lifestyle, we begin to become "partakers of the
divine nature" (2 Peter 1:4), and progressively become more like Christ
through becoming "changed into the same image from glory to glory, even
as by the
Spirit of the Lord" (2 Corinthians 3:18).

### 1. First be a child

*"Trust in the Lord with all thine heart; and lean not unto thine own
understanding. In all thy ways acknowledge him and he shall direct thy
paths."*
Proverbs 3:5,6

Each of us have numerous roles which we play in our day-to-day
lives. These include positions in our careers, in organizations, and even in
our family, such as spouse, mother, father, brother, sister, or child. The

extent to which we emphasize one role or another I believe has a profound influence on our sense of well-being. For example, when I become too caught up in my role as a psychologist, it is easy for me to become overly concerned, stressed, prideful, or any number of other unpleasant states of mind. I have also found that overemphasizing other roles, such as father or husband, eventually results in the same sense of being out of balance.

I have been experimenting with an approach which has been very helpful to me in better putting all of the various roles in context, which I call "First be a child." By this I mean, allowing a primary emphasis to be on my most basic role as an eternal child of God. This is not to diminish our role as children of an earthly father, but again to put that role into context in comparison to our more deep and satisfying position in relation to our Heavenly Father.

My young children, when they want or need attention from me, are very persistent. They ask repeatedly to play with them, hold them, and want to show me things that they have learned or made. They especially seem to want to begin a new day with close interactions, such as a hug or a kiss. As I begin a new day with an attitude of seeking a connection with my Heavenly Father, it is a humbling and peace promoting experience to better comprehend the reality that I am first and foremost a child, even though I may have "adult-like" responsibilities. The other roles then diminish, not in importance, but in the level of burden that is felt, realizing that I am not alone.

As a child, I have permission to do things that children do: Children smile; children try new things; they often do not succeed immediately at what they are doing, but they try again. Children also get excited about presents, which leads us to the next suggestion.

> You are as young as your faith, as old as your doubt, as young as your self-confidence, as old as your fear, as young as your hope, as old as your despair. In the central place of your heart, there is a recording chamber; so long as it receives messages of beauty, hope, cheer, and courage, so long you are young. When the wires are all down, and your heart is covered with the snow of pessimism and the ice of cynicism, then--and then only--are you grown old.
> General Douglas McArthur

## 2. Open the Presents

It has been said, "Yesterday is History. Tomorrow is a Mystery. Today is a gift--That's why we call it 'the Present'." Earlier in the book, it was discussed how the present seems to be our access to eternity where we can be influenced by the Fuel of Inspiration. The "gifts of the Spirit" such as faith, and discernment (see 1 Corinthians 12:4-11) are, of course, given by inspiration, and thus we can view the gifts as being available when we open our presents.

Let's imagine that there are 1000 moments in each day, with each of those moments being a "present." Or in other words, picture a huge pile of 1000 presents, and upon awakening, your task in any given day, it to see how many of those presents you can open! These are special presents, because each are unique to you. They may be full of surprises, but as each is opened and appreciated, they lead us to living a more abundant life. Each present is packaged with a small amount of Fuel of Inspiration, and as each present is opened, greater amounts of this fuel begins to warm our soul.

## 3. Don't Open Junk Mail Thoughts or Believe Tabloid Thinking

*"This I say therefore, and testify in the Lord, that ye henceforth walk not as other Gentiles walk, in the vanity of their minds. Having the understanding darkened, being alienated from the life of God through the ignorance that is in them because of the blindness of their heart. Who being past feeling have given themselves over to lasciviousness, to work all uncleanness with greediness."*
Ephesians 4:17-19

Just as it is important to live in the moment and open many presents each day, it is also important to practice not opening junk mail. By this I mean that we should avoid spending time with "junk mail thoughts." Junk mail thoughts, like actual junk mail, if opened and dwelt upon, can distract us, tempt us and complicate our lives.

I like to ask clients how they recognize a piece of junk mail when they sort through the items that arrive in their mailbox. They typically list certain characteristics, such as being addressed only to resident or occupant, having an envelope that is larger than normal, and having bright colors and sensational statements such as "FREE," "GUARANTEED!" or "CONGRATULATIONS!" With practice in identifying junk mail, we can easily and quickly sort our mail according to items we would like to spend time with, and items we would do well to simply discard.

So is it also with junk mail thoughts. With practice we can learn which thoughts are not worth listening to and should be discarded. This skill is part of spiritual discernment. The word "discernment" comes from the Greek word "diakrisis," which means the "act of separating apart." Some of the characteristics of such low quality thoughts, previously discussed, include agitation, increased self consciousness, and increased pressure.

The relative noisiness of these thoughts, just like loud colors typically found on items of junk mail, can help us to quickly identify them and discard them. Although we may not be able to totally stop junk mail being delivered to our mailbox, we can learn to not respond to it, and we can gradually at least reduce the amount we are receiving.

PRACTICAL EXERCISE

1. When you go to your mailbox in the near future, try quickly sorting your mail into piles of junk mail and non junk mail.

2. Then pick up the stack of junk mail and verbally state something like, "I'm not going to open you and I'm throwing you out!" as you throw the batch away.

3. On the same day as you do steps 1 & 2 above, listen carefully for a junk mail thought, consciously label it, and then get rid of it.

---

Yesterday is history.

Tomorrow is a mystery.

Today is a gift: that is why
we call it the present.

author unknown

---

112

Don't take the following too seriously:

Tabloids

Junk Mail

Agitated thoughts

Closely related to not opening junk mail thoughts, is the suggestion to not believe "Tabloid Thinking." As you know, tabloid newspapers can be found near the checkout counters in stores and have eye-catching sensational headlines. The themes of such newspapers range from bizarre to ridiculous, with a variety of dark and emotion laden topics. Unfortunately, not everything that is printed is true. Further, many things that are true, need not be focused on, and if we do, result in our mood sinking.

Just as certain things in print are not worth reading, certain thoughts are not worth thinking. "Tabloid Thinking" can be detected through recognizing when your train of thought is resulting in feeling agitated or otherwise playing on your emotions. This is a signal that such thinking is not to be fully believed. With increased exposure to such literature or thoughts, our sensitivity to appreciation of thoughts accompanied by peaceful feelings becomes reduced. In extreme situations, people lose their affinity to peaceful feelings (Ephesians 4:17-19), can have our "consciences seared with a hot iron" (1 Timothy 4:1,2) and only feel "alive" with progressively higher levels of emotional excitement.

A common feature of addiction or enslavement is an involvement with something related to our earthly bodies, earthy possessions or earthly accomplishments, which requires greater and greater levels of involvement to find a sense of excitement. In such states of mind, we are actually becoming increasingly dead to the Spirit, such that increasingly shocking or stimulating jolts are necessary to reach even a certain sense of aliveness.

### 4. Slow Down

*"Be still, and know that I am God."*
Psalms 46:10

Closely related to the previous suggestions is our need to slow down, usually both physically and mentally. Our modern insecurities manifest, in part, through the common belief that we can measure our worth by the busyness of our schedules or the number of tasks we have accomplished. Such a lifestyle essentially guarantees that we use man-made emotional fuels until they are depleted and we eventually become exhausted.

A slowing down of our mental activity involves allowing our mind to be quieter on a regular basis. Only when our own thoughts are allowed to drift away can the uplifting whisperings of the Spirit be detected. I believe that just as the sun is always shining, guidance and inspiration is always available as needed and as we reduce both physical and mental interferences. As an example of this, let me relate a fairly recent experience I had.

While my family and I were waiting to find our current home, we lived for four months in an apartment with the eight of us. It is a long standing joke in my family that Dad makes breakfast every morning, and always makes his favorite--oatmeal. One morning, while in the small kitchen of this apartment, I had turned on a tape to listen to some peaceful music, while preparing to make my favorite breakfast. After putting the salt and oatmeal into the boiling water, I became temporarily distracted and then heard the oatmeal boiling over onto the stove. I quickly moved the pot to another burner and then switched on the overhead exhaust fan to pull away the smoke from the burning oatmeal. While the fan continued whirling, I turned on the sink faucet to moisten a rag to clean up the mess. For several minutes, both the water and the overhead fan continued to run as I cleaned up my mess. I then turned off the faucet and had the faint experience of hearing something.

The overhead fan continued to run until the smoke had mostly cleared. As I switched off the fan and as its motor gradually quieted, out of the noise emerged the peaceful music from the tape player. I was impressed by the fact that it had been playing the whole time, but with those two sources of noise, I had not heard the music and had, in fact, forgotten that it was playing. When the fan had been running and the water turned off, I had a hint at a subliminal level of what I now know was the music, which only became fully discernible when the noise of the fan had also been eliminated. Often in our modern world, more than one source of noise needs to be reduced or eliminated in our lives in order to hear the subtle signals of the Spirit, which are always attempting to communicate with us.

PRACTICAL EXERCISE

Consider the man-made environments which have been created to lull people into using poor judgment or to not have the peaceable things of the Spirit be prevalent. A common feature of such settings, whether it is a carnival, casino, or bar, is the noise level.

Contrast your feelings and thoughts in a noisy setting, as opposed to a very peaceful one.

"Smart people spend time alone. They don't fill their days with appointments from 8 a.m. to 10 p.m., as many politicians and executives do. Great science does not emerge from hard logic and grinding hours.

It comes from the mysterious resources of the human brain and soul. Inspiration is nurtured by activities like chopping wood and raking leaves, preparing dinner and reading to the kids. These activities soften the rigid pace of the day's pursuits and allow all our God given intuition to work its unlogical magic. Only then can we reach our fullest potential. Only then can we leap from thinking to understanding."

Phillip K. Howard

## 5. Nature Nourishment

*"And God saw everything that he had made, and, behold, it was good."*

Genesis 1:31

Regular involvement with nature adds spiritual fuel to the lamp of our souls. For one thing, nature is usually more quiet and less rushed than man-made things. Nature, of course, was designed and created by God, and it has been said, "God made time, but man made haste" (Irish Proverb). Nature does not produce nor deliver junk-mail or tabloids, and thus our minds are less bombarded by agitated thoughts when in a more natural setting. Further, in natural settings,
our senses can be more healthily stimulated, which softens and opens our hearts. Several quotes presented below describe how involvement with nature and our senses brighten our souls

"Everything stress is, gardening is not. Stress is hurried and harried; gardening the pace of nature's season-long rhythms. Stress is feeling powerless and victimized; gardening is control over both your food supply and your immediate environment. Stress is alienation, isolation; gardening is taking part in the great cycles of the earth, the cycles of growth and nourishment, or death and rebirth, it is a daily and joyous ritual of participation in the unity of life. As you garden, you are healed--body and mind, heart and soul."

William Gottlieb

"Smell is a potent wizard that transports us across a thousand miles and all our years. The odors of fruit trees waft me to my Southern home, to frolics in the peach orchard. Other odors, instantaneous and fleeting, cause my heart to dilate joyously or contract with remembered grief. Even as I think of smells, my nose is full of scents that awake sweet memories of summers gone and ripening grain fields far away."

Helen Keller

## 6. Prayer Nourishment

*"For I know the thoughts that I think toward you, said the Lord, thoughts of peace, and not of evil, to give you an expected end. Then shall ye call upon me, and ye shall go and pray unto me, and I will hearken unto you. And ye shall seek me, and find me, when ye shall search for me with all your heart."*

Jeremiah 29:11-13

With the day being the basic unit of life, we should begin and end each day with communication with God, who is the source of all life. It is helpful in such prayers to be on our knees, in part to remind us that we are as a little child before God. Because he knows our needs better than we do, it is important to relax our minds, open our hearts, and let the influence of eternity come through our present moment. The Spirit can then guide us to know what to pray for, as we quietly listen for impressions to come to our hearts and minds. As we practice sincere and open hearted prayer, our faith can increase, because faith can only truly be experienced in the present as we humbly trust in the Lord.

Sometimes God
calms the storm--
and sometimes
he
lets the storm rage
and
calms his child.

author unknown

As we exercise such faith, it is as if we are exercising a stiff and unlimber part of our body. As the opening of our heart becomes more flexible and limber, the light rays of eternity are more able to be transmitted through us to both enlighten our vision and fill us with joy and peace. Prayer is not an activity based on logic or our human understanding, and can help us to experience the peace which passes understanding.

In addition to beginning and ending each day in sincere prayer, having a prayer continually in our heart throughout the day, is made more possible by increasing the number of moments we are in the present and thereby more in contact with eternity.

PRACTICAL EXERCISE

Practice having personal prayer in a quiet, unrushed setting where you are on your knees. Quiet your mind and imagine clouds parting to let sunrays come through. As you become calmer, your mood goes to higher levels where you can see things more clearly. Begin listening to and expressing the impressions, which gently come to your heart and mind.

## 7. Personal Scripture Nourishment

*"My son, attend to my words; incline thine ear unto my sayings. Let them not depart from thine eyes; keep them in the midst of thine heart. For they are life unto those that find them, and health to all their flesh."*
Proverbs 4:20-22

Daily personal study and pondering of the scriptures is a wonderful source of spiritual fuel for our individual lamps. Through a regular replenishing of such fuel, we maintain a higher level of peace, perspective and warmth.

Another aspect of personal scripture nourishment is that of memorizing passages to use when unpeaceful thoughts and emotions weigh us down. Chuck Swindoll, on a radio broadcast, gave three guidelines concerning memorizing and using verses, which I found very insightful:

118

1. Memorize when in a peaceful state of mind.

2. Rehearse them at peaceful times, frequently enough to have them crisp in your mind to call upon instantaneously.

3. Personalize the verse to you (e.g. "In God have I (put in your name) put my trust: I will not be afraid of what man can do unto me." Psalms 56:11).

I am impressed with how scriptures memorized in such a fashion are the perfect counteraction to unhealthy dark thoughts which may come along. Recall how it was discussed earlier that unhealthy and untrue thoughts have certain characteristics, including being pressure filled and agitated, noisy and nagging, plus seem to personally reflect on us through increased self consciousness. Those characteristics combine to have those thoughts be powerful in influencing us to believe them.

In the mental battle between true inspired thoughts and untrue and uninspiring thoughts, the peaceful state of mind anchored to a memorized verse counters the pressure filled and agitated aspect, the clear and crisp memorizing counters the noisy and nagging aspect, and by personalizing the verse, the distorted self consciousness of the dark thoughts can be countered. Thus the more a verse is peacefully and crisply memorized in a personalized way, the more it can be a highly effective tool in combating and replacing thoughts which darken our minds and make our hearts heavy.

## 8. Uplifting Music

*"Let the word of Christ dwell in you richly in all wisdom; teaching and admonishing one another in psalms and hymns and spiritual songs, singing with grace in your hearts to the Lord."*

Colossians 3:16

One of the last things Jesus did before going to the Garden of Gethsemane, to atone for our sins, was to sing a song with His disciples:

*"And when they had sung an hymn, they went out into the mount of Olives."*

Mark 14:26

Uplifting music can have a strong impact on strengthening us through affecting our feelings and our thoughts, thereby adding oil to our spiritual lamps.

The poet Longfellow stated, "Yet music is the prophet's art. Among the gifts that God has sent, one of the most magnificent." (Henry Wadsworth Longfellow, *Christus*). The famous composer, Johan Sebastian Bach, said, "Where there is devotional music, God is always at hand with His gracious presence," (Kavanaugh, *The Spiritual Lives of Great Composers*, p. 10). Inspiring music can literally lift our spirits to a higher plane with the accompanying feelings of joy, peace and good will toward men, just as the angels sang announcing the birth of Jesus (Luke 2:13-14)

Singing or playing uplifting music together with others is an especially enriching activity. Consider the impact of combining the use of your body, mental focus and feelings as you produce music in such a way as to put your whole soul into it. Further consider the unifying nature of participating with others in such a focus. Thoughts are less likely to wander while participating in music, thus bringing the hearts and minds of the participants together. If the music is Christ centered, the participants can then more fully be one with each other and with Christ.

While uplifting music allows our spirits to soar with greater perspective, compassion and peace, sensual music strongly influences our bodies and minds to have more narrow content, passion and emotional excitement. Certain types of music "harmonizes" with our particular mood level at any given time. This is important to know, so that if we recognize the "music in our heart," and if we are not content with our current level, we can listen to, sing or otherwise participate in music that can lift us.

Just as it is important to have favorite scripture versus crisply memorized, to replace unhealthy thoughts, so is it important to have hymns and other uplifting music memorized to help make our hearts more buoyant.

PRACTICAL EXERCISES

1. Memorize a favorite hymn or song to sing when feeling low.
2. Regularly sing or participate in uplifting music with others and be sensitive to the unifying nature of doing so.

## 9. Obey Commandments

*"Let thine heart retain my words; Keep my commandments and live.*

*But the path of the just is as the shining light, that shineth more and more unto the perfect day.*

*The way of the wicked is as darkness: they know not at what they stumble."*

Proverbs 4:4,18,19

Once we have heard the words of the Lord, whether through impressions in our hearts and minds through prayer, the scriptures or through inspired music, we need to then begin <u>doing</u> something about what we have heard. The apostle James said it concisely, when he encouraged followers of Christ, "But be ye <u>doers</u> of the word, and not hearers only, deceiving your own selves." (James 1:23, emphasis added). Similarly, the apostle John declared, "But he that <u>doeth</u> truth cometh to the light, that his deeds may be manifest, that they are wrought in God" (St. John 3:21, emphasis added).

As we obey the commandments, we come closer to the Light of Christ, as if we are growing closer to Him and becoming more one with Him. As we do so, our joy becomes more full and our vision more clear. This is stated beautifully in Psalms 19:8: "The statutes of the Lord is pure, enlightening the eyes."

Let's review and discuss some of the commandments briefly. Jesus was asked by a man, "Master, which is the great commandment in the law?" Jesus responded:

"Thou shalt love the Lord thy God with all thy heart, and with all thy soul, and with all thy mind."

Jesus then continued and said, "And the second is like unto it.

Thou shalt love thy neighbor as thyself. On these two commandments hang all the law and the prophets." (St. Matthew 22:36-40)     Let's examine the Ten Commandments in relation to these two commandments.

1. Thou shalt have no other gods before me.
2. Thou shalt not make unto thee any graven image.

121

3. Thou shalt not take the name of the Lord thy God in vain.
4. Remember the Sabbath day to keep it holy.
5. Honor thy father and thy mother.
6. Thou shalt not kill.
7. Thou shalt not commit adultery.
8. Thou shalt not steal.
9. Thou shalt not bear false witness against thy neighbour.
10. Thou shalt not covet thy neighbours house...nor anything that is thy neighbour's.

Exodus 20:3-17

Obeying each of the above ten commandments helps to add spiritual oil to our lamps, through placing God first and refining our lives so that we are more like Him. Although each of the ten commandments show our honor and love of God, the first four show our honor to Him more directly and the last six show our love through our behavior, in relation to His other children in our immediate surroundings.

It is interesting that eight of the ten commandments are guidelines of what not to do. When Jesus came to earth, he taught His disciples what to do, and explained, "Think not that I am come to destroy the law, or the prophets: I am not come to destroy, but to fulfil" (St. Matthew 5:17).

In contrast to the commandments describing what not to do, Jesus taught "higher" components of the laws of God, which are part of an active giving of ourselves:

*"A new commandment I give unto you, That ye love one another; as I have loved you, that ye also love one another."*

St. John 13:34      This

love of God abiding in our heart is like a direct pipeline of oil to the lamps of our souls.
Jesus said:

*"As the Father hath loved me, so have I loved you: continue in my love.*

*If ye keep my commandments, ye shall abide in my love, even as I have kept my Father's commandments, and abide in his love.*

*These things have I spoken unto you that my joy might remain in you, and that your joy might be full."*

St. John 15:9-11

## PRACTICAL EXERCISE

Prayerfully ponder as you read the higher portions of the law Jesus taught in St. Matthew chapters 5 and 6. Pay particular attention to Jesus' emphasis on active doing, and on the importance of our intentions, thoughts, emotions and feelings

### 10. Repent of wrongdoing

*"To give knowledge of salvation unto his people by the remission of their sins,*
*Through the tender mercy of our God; whereby the dayspring from on high hath visited us.*
*To give light to them that sit in darkness and in the shadow of death, to guide our feet into the way of peace."*
Luke 1:77-79

Each of us needs to repent and progressively do better at obeying the commandments.
*"For all have sinned, and come short of the glory of God"*
(Romans 3:23).
Even though the sun really is always shining, we separate ourselves from the warmth of God's love and guidance by our iniquities. This was described clearly by Isaiah:
*"Behold, the Lord's hand is not shortened, that it cannot save; neither his ear heavy, that it cannot hear:*
*But your iniquities have separated between you and your God, and your sins have hid his face from you, that he will not hear."*
Isaiah 59: 1,2
As a consequence of disobedience, the spiritual light can be blocked to the point where we may not be able to comprehend it.
*"We grope for the wall like the blind, and we grope as if we had not eyes: we stumble at noonday as in the night."*
Isaiah 59:10
*"And thou shalt grope at noonday as the blind gropeth in darkness, and thou shalt not prosper in thy ways."*
Deuteronomy 28:29

The "good news" is that God so loved the world that he sent his only begotten son (St. John 3:16) referred to as the "Son of righteousness" who shall arise with healing in his wings" (Malachi 4:2).

*"The people that walked in darkness have seen a great light; they that dwell in the land of shadow of death, upon them hath the light shined."*

Isaiah 9:2

*"To open their eyes, and to turn them from darkness to light, and from the power of Satan unto God, that they may receive forgiveness of sins."*

Acts 26:18

It is important to avoid accepting the standards of the world as appropriate, but hold firm to the standards of God, realizing that He will help us to overcome our weaknesses and mistakes.

*"And be not conformed to this world; but be ye transformed by the renewing of your mind, that ye may prove what is that good, and acceptable and perfect will of God."*

Romans 12:2

## 11. Taking Care of the Body

*"What? Know ye not that your body is the temple of the Holy Ghost which is in you, which ye have of God, and ye are not your own?*

*For ye are bought with a price; therefore glorify God in your body, and in your spirit, which are God's."*

1 Corinthians 6:19,20

I like to think of our body as a magnificent horse, with our spirit as the rider and trainer of the horse. Over time and experience we can learn to take care of the horse and train it to both submit to and work for the rider. This comparison of the body and spirit as horse and rider becomes graphic in the case of a rodeo. In the event of bronco riding, a huge horse bucks, kicks and attempts to throw off the rider. The rider is definitely not in charge, but simply is holding on for dear life. Such is the case when the influence of the body is dominating the influence of the spirit. In contrast, the rodeo events of calf roping or barrel racing are examples of the precision cooperation between horse and rider, comparable to the body being in submission to and in service of the spirit.

As we take care of our bodies, we add oil to our spiritual lamps and feel more fully alive. One of the most basic ways to take care of our bodies is to deeply breathe. As mentioned earlier in the book, the Latin word "spirare," from which we get the English word "spirit", means "to breathe." One of the most natural and enjoyable ways of breathing deeply is through exercise on a regular basis. Knowing that exercise has a strong influence on our inner well-being can be an additional incentive for regular exercise.

Of course, a variety of body care behaviors combine to help us be more energetic and resilient to disease. Some of these major factors are diet, rest, exercise, and avoidance of harmful substances.

The role of antidepressants and other medications for mental and emotional problems will be briefly discussed. Hormones and other body chemicals can become out of balance and medications can often assist in restoring a more proper balance. Only in extreme situations would an individual need to be on such medications for extended periods of time. Antidepressants, for example, could be compared to a cast on a broken leg, which is necessary as a temporary support as the natural forces of the body are healing the injury.

In depression, which includes much difficulty sleeping, one of the most helpful things that an antidepressant can do is allow for better rest. Such better sleep patterns alone can do wonders for a person's sense of clarity and hopefulness.

Medications should always be part of an overall program of care, including exercise, not dwelling on distorted thoughts, and the other points outlined in this book. For those individuals who seem to require medications on a more ongoing basis, the more they are involved in healthy patterns of living, the greater the possibility that their medications could, at least, be reduced as more natural healing forces are utilized.

PRACTICAL EXERCISE

Develop a routine of physical exercise at least 3 times per week for 20 minutes, which allows you to breathe deeply.

PERSONAL NOTES

# Chapter 10

## *Letting Your Light Shine*

*"Ye are the light of the world. A city that is set on a hill cannot be hid.*
*Neither do men light a candle, and put it under a bushel,*
*but on a candlestick; and it giveth light unto all that are in the house.*
*Let your light so shine before men, that they may see your good works, and*
*glorify your father which is in heaven."*

St. Matthew 5:14-16

When Thomas Edison harnessed electricity in the light bulb, he helped to bring light into homes around the world. As we individually learn to harness the Light of Christ in our hearts and minds, we can bring spiritual light to those around us.

It is important to emphasize that the light referred to throughout this book is a gift from God and evidence of his power and glory. This allows us to be both grateful for the light and warmth, while at the same time humble in knowing its source. The apostle Paul commented on giving God the credit for the light: "For God, who commanded the light to shine out of darkness hath shined in our hearts, to give the light of the knowledge of the glory of God in the face of Jesus Christ. But we have this treasure in earthen vessels, that the excellency of the power may be of God and not of us" (2 Corinthians 3:6,7).

The chief lesson of my life to this point is my dependence on the Lord. I have learned that me by myself is <u>nothing</u>, that God by himself is <u>everything</u>, and that me with God is <u>something</u>.

In addition to having our light shine to give glory to our Father in Heaven, the introductory scripture of this chapter mentions giving light to all that are in the house. I like to think of the reference to the house as an indicator that God wants us to be a tool in His hands, primarily for the family and the immediate environment in which He placed us. I believe such priorities are in harmony with what Jesus described as the first great commandments: "Thou shalt love the Lord by God with all thy heart, and with all thy soul, and with all thy mind. This is the first and great commandment. And the second is like unto it, Thou shalt love thy neighbor as thyself" (St. Matthew 22:37-39).

When my family and I lived in Iowa and would travel to Sioux Falls, South Dakota, we would pass a series of billboard-like signs along the highway. One I especially liked read simply: Think Globally, Act Locally. Such a view reminds me of the scene in the movie, "Gandhi," in which a young man enthusiastically approaches Gandhi, expressing how he

128

had felt enlightened and was seeking a grand assignment in the national movement Gandhi was leading. The young man seemed disillusioned when Gandhi congratulated him on his enlightenment and enthusiasm and then said, "Go home and help your neighborhood." Similarly, Mother Theresa has said, "There are no great deeds, only small deeds done with great love."

Consistent with the above messages, in this final chapter a number of small actions will be discussed, with the hope that we can intensify the love associated with such actions through using the principles presented in the book.

### 1. Let your light shine with a smile.

"A smile is a light in the window of the soul indicating that the heart is at home"
(Author unknown).

Nothing on earth can make life
more worthwhile.
Than a true, loyal friend and
the warmth of a smile --
For, just like a sunbeam makes cloudy days brighter.
The smile of a friend makes
a heavy heart lighter.

Helen Steiner Rice

### 2. Let your light shine with soft and cheerful words.

*"A soft answer turneth away wrath, but grievous words stir up anger."*

Proverbs 15:1

*"Heaviness in the heart of man maketh it stoop: but a good word maketh it glad."*

Proverbs 12/25

I would like to relate a story of how my wife let her light shine in helping dispel a dark state I was in. All of us lose our bearings at times; and, after my wife and I had been learning some of these principles, I was coming home from work one day after having lost my bearings. As I drove home, I was full of pressure and saw the world as a bleak place and I was certainly feeling no better about myself. I entered the house in a huff, and my wife was doing something in the kitchen and in a very cheerful, lighthearted voice said, "Hi honey." I thought to myself, "Hi honey? Where in the world is she coming from? Doesn't she know how bleak things are?" I said something grumpy, and I cannot actually recall now whether she said something cheerful back or simply did not respond and

129

went cheerfully about whatever she was doing. Well, I could see that we were not connecting, so went on my grumpy way toward the bedroom.

Without me knowing it, my wife had planted a "seed of doubt" in my mind that what I was seeing was not the whole picture. I did not know this at the time, but when I went into the bedroom, that seed began to take root; and, as I put my briefcase down and took my tie off, I stopped thinking about whatever I had been thinking. The pressure seemed to lift somewhat, and I walked out a few moments later to talk with my wife.

I said to her, "I came home in kind of a grumpy mood." "Yeah, I know," she stated matter-of-factly. I then questioningly stated, "Well you didn't attempt to comfort me or talk with me about it or..." She paused and, with a smile, simply said, "I trust your health."

This was a powerful example to me that my wife was able to help me overcome an insecure and low mood state, not by joining me there, but being a vivid example of contrary evidence. This contrary evidence is a powerful means of showing another in a lower mood state that they are not seeing the whole picture at the instant of dark perspective.

When a person is feeling the joy and exuberance of healthy well-being, he or she has a keen trust in the ability of others to also be healthy. As the resonance of health is diminished, the sense of confidence in others being able to be healthy is correspondingly decreased. In lower mood functioning, the human tendency is to feel the need to force others out of a bad mood because they certainly do not seem to have the ability to do it themselves!

Faking being in a good mood, in an attempt to help another out of a lower mood state, simply does not have the same effect as genuine experience of healthy functioning. There certainly must be some kind of unconscious communication which takes place that reflects your trust in the health of the other and thereby provides powerful contrary evidence to the less than full perspective being experienced by the other.

### 3. Let your light shine by expressing gratitude.
*"And let the peace of God rule in your hearts, to the which also ye are called in one body, and be ye thankful."*
Colossians 3:15

I came home from work one evening in a good mood and grateful to be home. I was disappointed to find that one of my children, a seven year old boy, had been sent to bed for getting really upset and punching his next older brother. As I went up to his room, I found him sitting up in the bed, with the covers over his legs and his back against the wall, with an angry scowl on his face. Attempting to comfort him, I said, "What's the matter pal?" He replied in a grumpy voice, "I ate a fly!" "You ate a fly?" I exclaimed.  He went on to explain that he had been licking one of the beaters my wife had used in making a chocolate cake.  He had not known that a fly was stuck to the beater, and as he licked, the fly and the batter went down his throat.  He probably would not have even known the difference, had his brother not watched and pointed out too late what was going on.

This led to my seven year old (who has a hard time eating anything crunchy) having a gag reflex and the brother laughing at his dilemma.  Feeling very self-conscious and with his feelings hurt, the seven year old did what came naturally and socked his brother.

Thank goodness I was in a good mood, not to mention the humor I saw in the situation.  Had I not been in a good mood, I might have taken the situation very seriously and attempted to "solve and end the problem," by angrily getting after the older brother.  Instead, the thought occurred to me to ask my son, "Did you eat any batter?"  He raised his eyes to look at me, while maintaining a scowl on his face, and said, "Well, yes."  I then asked, "Which did you have more of--the fly or the batter?"  Now he was really wondering where I was coming from, dropped the scowl from his face and looked at me inquisitively and quietly stated, "batter."  I then hammed it up a little and said, "Well this is really strange.  We could be talking about all that batter that you ate and here we are talking about that little ol' fly."

Love is something eternal--the aspect may change, but not the essence.  There is the same difference in a person before and after he is in love, as there is in an unlighted lamp and one that is burning.
The lamp was there and it was a good lamp, but now it is shedding light, too, and that is its real function.

Vincent Van Gogh

An interesting part of life is the fact that small negative things can capture our attention much more dramatically than a large quantity of more peaceful and pleasant things. This is an example of how, when negative emotions are involved, our thoughts become charged, or energized, to the point of becoming blown up in importance. Or, in other words, negative emotions tend to imprint the thoughts associated with them more deeply in our awareness.

On the other hand, thoughts when we are experiencing pleasure or contentment are quiet, to the point of us not even being aware that we are thinking. I wonder if this is why we have the urge to grab the camera when an especially warm or pleasant scene is being witnessed. It is as if without a means of capturing the experience, it will fade away, as do most peaceful thoughts. We need picture albums to remind us of the happy times. In contrast, negatively charged thoughts and memories need no reminders; they speak for themselves. Therefore it is especially important to frequently express gratitude to each other for little kindnesses.

### 4. Let your light shine by listening.

It is interesting that many activities, which are healthy for us, allow us to be more fully alive while, at the same time, helping another to be more fully alive also. Active listening is one of the cornerstones of uplifting relationships, whether in our everyday interactions or in professional therapy.

When I think of the importance of listening, I often think of the famous psychiatrist, Karl Menninger, who, along with his father and brother, helped to found the Menninger Clinic in Topeka, Kansas. I had heard that he often repeated his encouragement to other mental health professionals: "Listen to your patients. Listen to your patients." In June, 1990, my family and I drove from our hometown of Cherokee, Iowa, to Topeka, Kansas, for me to attend a workshop at the Menninger Clinic, while my family visited friends in Topeka. In the late afternoon, after the conclusion of the workshop, I set about to hopefully fulfill a desire I had to meet and briefly speak with Karl Menninger, who I learned was still living and, although in his nineties, still frequently worked in his office on the campus of the Menninger Clinic.

While my family waited in the car, I went to the administration building and expressed my desire. You can imagine my excitement when I was invited to enter his office and was able to meet this kindly legend in the mental health field. Wanting to hear his famous encouragement from his own mouth, I asked if there was any particular advice he had for me as a young mental health professional. He then said what I had hoped I would hear and admonished me to listen, really listen to the people I work with. He then practiced what he preached and asked me about my life circumstances, which allowed me to tell him of my wife and, at that time, five sons. He seemed joyfully impressed with that and said that I must have an especially brave wife.

At that point, I realized how much my wife would enjoy meeting him and asked if I might have her come in while I stayed with the children in the car. He visited with her longer than he had with me, and she came out beaming with a copy of one of his books, which he had signed.

I was interested to look in the index of the book to see what he might have written in it, concerning listening, and found a delightful section including Dr. Menninger quoting another, in what he felt at the time, was the best description he had read concerning the power of listening in helping be more alive.

"A good many hundreds of pages have been written about this attentive listening in the technical literature, but I do not recall anything else so eloquent and, at the same time, so sound as an article by Brenda Ueland, published not in the Psychoanalytic Review, not in the American Journal of Psychiatry, not in the Journal of American Medical Association (where perhaps it should have been), but in the Ladies Home Journal! In the issue for November 1941, Miss Ueland writes:

Listening is a magnetic and strange thing, a creative force...The friends that listen to us are the ones we move toward, and we want to sit in their radius as though it did us good, like ultraviolet rays...When we are listened to, it creates us, makes us unfold and expand. Ideas actually begin to grow within us and come to life...It makes people happy and free when they are listened to...When we listen to people there is an alternating current and this recharges us so that we never get tired of each other. We are constantly being recreated.

Now there are brilliant people who cannot listen much. They have no ingoing wires on their apparatus. They are entertaining but exhausting too. I think it is because of these lecturers, these brilliant performers, by not giving us a chance to talk, do not let us express our thoughts and expand; and it is this expressing and expanding that makes the little creative fountain inside us begin to spring and cast up new thoughts and unexpected laughter and wisdom.

I discovered all this about three years ago, and truly it made a revolutionary change in my life. Before that, when I went to party, I would think anxiously: 'Now try hard. Be lively. Say bright things. Talk. Don't let down.' And when tired, I would have to drink a lot of coffee to keep this up. But now, before going to party, I just tell myself to listen with affection to anyone who talks to me, to be in their shoes when they talk; to try to know them without my mind pressing against their, or arguing, or changing the subject.  No.  My attitude is: Tell me more.  This person is showing me his soul.  It is a little dry and meager and full of grinding talk just now, but presently he will begin to think, not just automatically to talk.  He will show his true self.  Then he will be wonderfully alive"...(*Love Against Hate*, p. 275-276, 1942).

Perhaps this would be an appropriate place to briefly discuss interacting with teenagers.  One of the most frequent complaints from teenagers is "Nobody listens to me!"  The next couple of pages are for parents or others who interact frequently with teenagers.

The teenage years are a time of tremendous change, which is not only confusing for parents, but also for the teenagers themselves.  Physically, they are going through puberty with the accompanying growth spurts and sexual maturation.  The human brain, which is not mature until about age 22, is also undergoing many changes.  One of these changes involves the maturing of connections in the brain, which allows the reasoning centers to inhibit the messages from the emotional centers.  Until those pathways are well developed, the emotional centers of the brain are free to send impulsive and irrational messages, which if followed, results in immature behavior.

Looking at interpersonal factors, teenagers are in the throws of forming their identity, trying to prove their adequacy among their peers, and awkwardly both wanting and being afraid of independence from parents.  Sometimes adolescent rebellion can be related, at least in part, to an attempt to not grow up and be part of adulthood, which is seen by some teenagers as synonymous with boredom and drudgery.

Many psychological factors are also changing, including a growing ability to comprehend multiple viewpoints on a given topic.  More concrete black-and-white reasoning begins to give way to considering other viewpoints, which can also result in questioning their parents' values and rules.  This is all taking place in a society of unstable and changing values.  Combine all these factors, and no wonder the teenage years can be a time of turmoil.  But there is hope.  If turmoil is the problem, then I would like to suggest that the solution is **PEACE**.  (Patience, Example, Attitude, Caring & Courage, and Evidence).

**Patience:**  The last chapter has not yet been written.  Do not let worrying about the future crowd out the natural wisdom you have as a parent to deal with the current situation.

**Example:**  There are three ways to teach--example, example, example.  Show your teenager by example that adulthood is an interesting place by developing a satisfying and well-rounded lifestyle, including hobbies, fun and other things to be more fully alive. This helps give them hope to keep paddling toward the shores of adulthood.

**Attitude:** When you are personally enjoying life, your health brings a lighter mood in the family. Where mood is low and heavy, I.Q. is also low. As parents, if we are brighter and have a sense of humor, somehow solutions are more easily visible.

**Caring and Courage:** Teenagers need and (deep inside) want firm limits placed upon them by people they know really care. Small acts of acceptance and devotion demonstrate love, as does the courage to have firm limits and consequences. Teenagers are experts at insecurity and are comforted to be around the strong security of love and limits.

**Evidence:** Keep a keen eye out for evidence of the strengths and goodness in your child. They are still in there and you can see them come up for air now and then. When we are personally more in touch with our own health, we are better able to see and appreciate strengths in our children--even teenagers!

### 5. Let your light shine by forgiving.

*"He that saith he is in the light, and hateth his brother, is in darkness even until now.*
*He that loveth his brother abideth in the light, and there is none occasion of stumbling in him.*
*But he that hateth his brother is in darkness, and walketh in darkness, and knoweth not whither he goeth, because the darkness hath blinded his eyes."*

1 John 2:9-11

*"God is light, and in him is no darkness at all.*
*If we say that we have fellowship with him, and walk in darkness, we lie, and do not the truth.*
*But as we walk in the light as he is in the light, we have fellowship one with another."*

1 John 1:5-7

Some of the most tender scenes in the Bible are concerning people lovingly reconciling their differences. There is probably nothing more divine than forgiving another and coming again to a close relationship. Consider both the warmth and the similarities in the following three accounts.

1. Jacob and his brother Esau after years of being separated following hard feelings:

*"And Esau ran to meet him, and embraced him, and fell on his neck and kissed  him: and they wept."*

Genesis 33:4

2.  Joseph being reconciled with his brothers who had sold him into slavery:

*"And he fell upon his brother Benjamin's neck, and wept, and Benjamin wept upon his neck.*
*Moreover he kissed all his brethren, and wept upon them: and after that his brethren talked with him."*

Genesis 46:14,15

3.  The prodigal son being reconciled with his father:

*"And he arose, and came to his father.  But when he was yet a great way off,  his father saw him, and had compassion, and ran, and fell on his neck, and kissed him."*

St. Luke 15:19

We can have strong positive influence on others around us as we have the Light of Christ burning in our hearts and minds and act in loving and forgiving ways.  A client of mine recently described, in a simple and profound way, how this process works.  The female client quoted a friend of hers who said, "When you know something is right, just live it, and it's not your job to make it a reality in other people's lives.  You just live it, and it's God's responsibility to make it a reality in their lives.  He uses examples to teach people, and you can be the example by living it."

Nothing feels more wonderful than the love of God.  I hope that the concepts and suggestions in this book can help us and others to experience that love more fully and frequently.

*"And the peace of God which passeth all understanding, shall keep your hearts and minds through Jesus Christ.*

*Finally brethren, whatsoever things are true, whatsoever things are honest, whatsoever things are just, whatsoever things are pure, whatsoever things are lovely, whatsoever things are of good report; if there be any virtue, and if there be any praise, think on these things."*

Philippians 4:7,8

*"That he would grant you, according to the riches of his glory, to be strengthened with might by his Spirit in the inner man;*

*That Christ may dwell in your hearts by faith; that ye, being rooted and grounded in love,*

*May be able to comprehend with all saints what is the breadth, and length, and depth, and height;*

*And to know the love of Christ, which passeth knowledge, that ye might be filled with all the fullness of God."*

Ephesians 3:16-19

# ENDORSEMENTS

"The Sun Is Always Shining is a great representation of Dr. Hulbert's mission, and when I was introduced to its first few pages, I knew it was a gem. In it, Dr. Hulbert shares practical examples that teach the reader their heroic potential, based on his years of experience as a Psychologist. This book is also filled with inspirational quotes and scriptures from the Holy Bible, serving as a wonderful resource for my personal use."

Ramsey Cooper<br>
New Vision Church<br>
New Members Orientation Leader<br>
Dickinson, Texas

"This extraordinary masterpiece is a wake-up call for those of us who are forward and strategic thinkers, as we explore options in making the world a better place. Thank you Dr. Ryan Hulbert for stirring up the passion within ourselves for the future, while looking at the SUN."

Suzanne Mayo, Ph.D.<br>
President/CEO, Mynette Management Company

"Our moods, feelings, and emotions tell us something about our relationships with God. Dr. Ryan Hulbert has provided a helpful process by which we can process the meaning of the impact on our soul, mind and spirit and navigate our journey toward wholeness. I would recommend *The Sun Is Always Shining* to anyone who is serious about their spiritual development."

Dr. Owen C. Cardwell, Jr., PhD<br>
www.heroesanddreamsacademy.org

"Your book is amazing! It is both therapeutic and healing at the same time. Reading the book is such an encouraging experience, which spontaneously ministers and induces a higher level of understanding, concerning mental and emotional health. This book presents higher techniques for ministering healing and promoting spiritual wholeness. I couldn't stop reading it, because throughout the book I saw God, hope, and actual healing through ministry. This book is revolutionary and I will recommend it to friends, family and all of my contacts."

Anita L. Poole<br>
Youth Advocate

"Having spent over 25 years in leadership, I find Dr. Ryan Hulbert's book, *The Sun Is Always Shining*, an excellent resource for mentoring, guiding and encouraging others. Dr. Hulbert skillfully illustrates how the word of God is the best response to life's problems and conflicts. You will experience clarity and a sense of well being on every page. A must read to experience inner peace."

Cheryl Beausoleil
President and CEO, Superior Integrated Home Health Care, INC

"Just a note to thank you for writing your book, *The Sun Is Always Shining*. I found so much help in overcoming my problems. Your ideas were new to me. I was convinced that I had to still the "busyness of mind" that has plagued me in the present moment (because the present is where eternity is). Your stories and illustrations gently opened my understanding. I have read a number of self help books, but these concepts have influenced me to the core of my being. In fact, the change has been so dramatic, that I was asked to teach a class on Stress and Goal Setting in my church. I thank you again for your preparation, inspiration, and willingness to share. It has changed my life."

Barbara Honn

"Per our discussion, I would like to order 10 copies of *The Sun Is Always Shining*. I look forward to receiving them very soon. My daughter feels this has made a great change in her life. I want to present a copy to each of my children, and she will present one to each of hers."

Kathleen M. Moore

"Thanks for your insightful writing! *The Sun Is Always Shining* offers a ray of hope for those stumbling in the darkness of emotional trauma. Dr. Hulbert addresses the connection between loving God and the healing process, and shows how the light of Christ positively empowers thought, feeling and mood. The result...a guide to experiencing a renewal of self-worth, spiritual well-being and psychological health. I will continue prescribing this to my patients, students and soldiers who are seeking heart-felt healing."

W. Sidney Young, Ph.D.
Psychological Counseling Services
Institute of Religion Instructor, USAR Chaplain

"I am thrilled to be able to purchase 5 more of your book, *The Sun Is Always Shining*. I have read and identified with it and many things are falling into place. Ideas are clearer in my thoughts and doors and windows have been unlocked and are swinging wide open. I feel my soul has been touched deeply and many of my anxieties healed. I have shared many things from your book with others, especially my adult children, and will continue to do so. Thank you again, and God bless your efforts."
Karen Fitch

*The Sun Is Always Shining* is a masterful piece of work. It illuminates the possibilities for a healthy, positive emotional state, which of course follows our thinking. I savored Ryan Hulbert's words and all of the other quotes of inspiration, as well as the scriptural content. This is a book that brightened each day as I read and contemplated it."
John Roberts
Author and Spiritual Counselor
Leadership Trainer and Executive Coach

"Your concepts and book have been very helpful at this and at my last command. I am currently located in Okinawa, with a total of about 40,000 military and about an equal number of military dependents. *The Sun Is Always Shining* brings light, not only to the counselees, but to the leaders. It gives them both a hope filled, spiritual approach to this temporary mortal experience in our spiritual journey. And, around here, people are way outside Jerusalem and wandering around in the desert. At my last duty station, the Alcohol Rehab Department of the San Diego Naval Medical Center, I used the How Much Truth Do We Perceive illustration with the incoming and later the patients at the three week point, to reinforce how their perception, hope and overall experience was going. They especially appreciated comparing where they were spiritually when they arrived with where they were after three weeks of intense work. I greatly appreciate the book. It, outside the scriptures, is my number one resource in my current assignment."
Steve Lineback, CAPT, USU, CHC

"I've started to read your book and your insight is so amazing. The way you have put things has hit a cord in my heart. It was like a light went on and things made sense."
Shellise Sharp

"I teach at a Senior Citizens Center and I teach a parenting class at a hospital. I use *The Sun Is Always Shining* as a resource for those classes and also in my private therapy. The book is simple, the principles are very clear, and it has even been helpful for people that may not believe in God."

June Bullock

Registered Nurse and Counselor

"Ryan does a masterful job in defining the three levels of human functioning in a caring, direct, and simple way. His personal examples provide us with great insight into our own lives and with an understanding of ways in which we can "hold to the rod." My own personal understanding of myself, my relationship to my family, and to the purpose of this life is more clearly defined as a result of my reading of this very effective work."

Gary M. Lloyd, Ed.D.

Former Executive Director,

Utah Center for Families in Education

Utah State Office of Education

Made in the USA
San Bernardino, CA
05 July 2019